W9-AZJ-305

The Professional Development Toolbox
Unlocking Simple Truths

Martin Klubeck

No part of this publication may be reproduced or transmitted in any form or by any means, mechanical or electronic, including photocopying and recording, or by any information storage and retrieval system, without permission in writing from the author.

The Professional Development Toolbox: Unlocking Simple Truths

Copyright © 2014 by Martin Klubeck

This work is subject to copyright. All rights are reserved by the author, whether the whole or part of the material is concerned, specifically the rights of translation, reprinting, reuse of illustrations, recitation, broadcasting, reproduction on microfilms or in any other physical way, and transmission or information storage and retrieval, electronic adaptation or by similar or dissimilar methodology now known or hereafter developed. Exempted from this legal reservation are brief excerpts in connection with reviews or scholarly analysis or materials supplied specifically for the purpose of being entered and executed on a computer system, for exclusive use by the purchaser of the work. Duplication of this publication or parts thereof is permitted only under the provisions of the Copyright Law of the Publisher's location, in its current version, and permission for use must always be obtained from the author. Permissions for use may be obtained by contacting the author at mkknowledgebuilders.com

Trademarked names, logos, and images may appear in this book. These references are only used in an editorial fashion and to the benefit of the trademark owner, with no intention of infringement of the trademark.

The use in this publication of trade names, trademarks, service marks, and similar terms, even if they are not identified as such, is not to be taken as an expression of opinion as to whether or not they are subject to proprietary rights.

While the advice and information in this book are believed to be true and accurate at the date of publication, neither the authors nor the editors nor the publisher can accept any legal responsibility for any errors or omissions that may be made. The publisher makes no warranty, express or implied, with respect to the material contained herein.

Publisher: Createspace Independent Publishing Platform
Editor: Michael Langthorne
Reviewers: Claire Noble, Nancy Studebaker
Artist: Martin Klubeck
Cover Designer: Martin Klubeck
Cover Model: Grace Klubeck

To all those struggling to improve their organizations, their processes, or themselves. Use your resources to develop your greatest asset, it'll pay dividends in the end.

To my children: I love you all. My most ardent wish is that you find love, joy, and happiness.

About the Author

Martin Klubeck is a strategy and planning consultant at the University of Notre Dame and a recognized expert in Organizational Development. He holds a master's degree from Webster University in human resources development and a bachelor's in computer science from Chapman University. He also has an associate's degree in Instructions systems development from the Community College of the Air Force.

He is the author of Metrics: How to Improve Key Business Results (Apress 2011) and a coauthor of Why Organizations Struggle So Hard to Improve So Little (Praeger 2009). His passion for simplifying the complex has led to the development of simple systems for organizational development including professional development, metrics, vision setting, and strategic planning.

The only thing Klubeck loves more than helping others implement organizational development improvements is his family. He is the proud father of three. Each of his children; Kristopher, Alyssa, and Grace exemplify solid and honorable core values. They are by far his greatest accomplishments.

Acknowledgements

As with any labor of love I've ever embarked upon, it feels like those who contributed their time, encouragement, and expertise did more to accomplish this work than I did.

The initial and consistent encouragement of my editor, Michael Langthorne was just the catalyst I needed, when I needed it to get me started on this effort. Sometimes we create things because it's how we make a living – each book I've written has been an answer to a calling. Mike was the first to alert me to the siren ringing in my ears.

My other cheer leader would be better described as a barometer of common sense and rational thinking. That's a nice way to say Don Padgett has a way of keeping any semblance of an ego I might have well in check. He keeps me humble, and for that I will be forever grateful.

I also want to acknowledge anyone and everyone who helped by reading my numerous drafts and providing feedback, especially Claire and Nancy. I also want to thank Kaye and Laura for testing parts of the practicum. Thanks!

This was a labor of love. I love helping others, especially with organizational development efforts. In Why Organizations Struggle so Hard to Improve so Little: Overcoming Organizational Immaturity (Praeger 2009) Michael, Don and I introduced a critical concept for organizational development. In it we touched on many mature behaviors which an organization struggling with Organizational Immaturity might not be able to address. Knowing that these behaviors are invaluable, I felt compelled to share the simple and practical ways I found to carry them out. That led to my writing Metrics: How to Improve Key Business Results (Apress 2011). A book on how to create development plans for employees, management, leadership, entrepreneurs, and even players on a sports team – truly anyone – was the logical follow on. I spent many years in the US Air Force writing courseware, developing training modules, and managing individual training programs. At the center of all of these efforts was the development plan. That foundation combined with over twenty years of experience in organizational development has culminated in this work.

I hope you enjoy it. And more importantly, I hope you use it.

Contents

About the Author v

Acknowledgements.. vii

Foreword...1

Prologue 5

PART ONE Laying the foundation...11

Chapter 1-1 Organized sports is big business 13

Chapter 1-2 The professional development plan.....................35

Chapter 1-3 How to use this book...45

PART TWO Concepts, Theories, and Principles.........................49

Chapter 2-1 The Master Task Listing (MTL) 51

Chapter 2-2 Define Training Requirements 69

Chapter 2-3 Determine required skill levels 89

Chapter 2-4 Evaluate existing abilities 97

Chapter 2-5 Gap management...109

Chapter 2-6 Selecting training vehicles.................................119

Chapter 2-7 Scheduling, assessing, and tracking training 129

Chapter 2-8 Benefiting from the information 143

Chapter 2-9 Bonus Material 157

Chapter 2-10 RECAP 163

PART THREE Practicum – Do It Yourself Development Planning 167

Chapter 3-1 The Master Task List...169

Chapter 3-2 Define Training Requirements 187

Chapter 3-3 Determine required skill levels 195

Chapter 3-4 Evaluate existing abilities..................................199

Chapter 3-5 Managing the Gap..203

Chapter 3-6 Selecting Training Vehicles................................205

Chapter 3-7 Scheduling, assessing, and tracking training.......................207

Chapter 3-8 A Sport Walkthrough...211

Chapter 3-9 A Business Position Walkthrough 225

Chapter 3-10 Bonus Material...233

Table of Figures

Figure 1, for tracking status of training scheduled/received..................139

Figure 2, for evaluating skill/knowledge level 140

Figure 3, sample of a chart for analysis of training evaluation...............141

Figure 4, sample table...188

Figure 5, determining training requirements 191

Figure 6, frequency and criticality...192

Figure 7, Attribute Analysis...193

Figure 8, sample scores..196

Figure 9, sample scores..201

Figure 10, sample scores..202

Figure 11, sample scores..203

Figure 12, sample scores..204

Figure 13, four attributes..217

Figure 14, attribute analysis..218

Figure 15, required assessment 219

Figure 16, skill assessment...220

Figure 17, gap analysis with priority 222

Figure 18, tracking training 224

Figure 19, business task attributes 228

Figure 20, business tasks analysis 229

Figure 21, business task requirement analysis 230

Foreword

Coaches by nature are competitive. We can't help ourselves.

And logically, we wouldn't have it any other way. Most of us are continually seeking ways to build a better mousetrap. While we readily "steal" ideas from each other, no treachery is required. Our profession has the odd quirk that while we're trying to beat our opponents into submission, we're quite willing to share our ideas with those same coaches that we spend hours scheming against.

You would think this wouldn't happen, especially since we are hired *and fired* for our ability to compete against teams from other colleges and universities from all over the United States. The thing is, we're not actually hired or fired for our ability to win, but instead for our ability to take a group of young men or women and mold them into a unit capable of winning. This may seem like a nuance, but it's much more.

My job as the head coach for the University of Notre Dame's Men's Tennis team wasn't to win or even compete. It was to develop the young men on my team.

I found that the ability to select, organize, and develop the talents of a group of young athletes is frequently the difference between just getting by and experiencing success at the highest level. This was certainly true in my personal experience.

When I arrived at Notre Dame our team was not even close to being nationally ranked. The goals and desires of the players on our team were neither unified nor were they even pointing in the same direction. Somehow, with more than a little luck involved, we were able to work our way up the ranks until in my fifth season we reached the NCAA finals, competing for the National Championship on the last day of the season in 1992. You would think reaching the finals was the highlight of my career at that time. But it wasn't.

When we lost to Stanford that day I was genuinely pleased. Not with losing – remember, I was and am very competitive. No, what pleased me was the way our guys competed and fought both *for and alongside each other.* We had completed the journey from irrelevant to the top of the mountain. Each of us had been forced to swallow his own selfish pride at times along the way and to demonstrate that we were there for each other, no matter the obstacle.

This growth required change. Even though by definition our players were amateurs, they had to develop professionally. Professional development is about growing in our chosen fields of expertise.

For me, this development is the central focus of what being a coach is all about.

Marty Klubeck gets that.

Marty is the perfect person to write a how-to book on professional development. I believe his career in the United States Air Force uniquely prepared him for this task. It is what our military does. Lessons about teamwork, accountability, and achievement are the mantra. Marty worked from Basic Airmen through the ranks and finally spanning the gap into the Officer corps. His own career was one of continuous improvement and professional development. His success may have been due to his competitive nature which I've seen demonstrated in his love of athletics and sport. He has become involved with some of the Notre Dame teams and has studied how coaches achieve success. Marty is a regular at our Eck Tennis Pavilion where he plays weekly with a group of players who compete and have fun doing it. But he can't help himself. He won't stop striving to improve. He frequently stops in my office on his way to play, sometimes for only a brief moment of conversation and other times for extended dialogues. In most of these discussions, he ends up picking my brain about how he can improve. From equipment questions to specific skill improvement – he is pleasant and inquisitive.

He is infectiously enthusiastic, whether about his new racket or improved backhand ground stroke, but never dull. And I was not surprised to find that he writes with the same energy and enthusiasm.

I have enjoyed my talks with Marty. One of the things I like the most is hearing about his experiences with developing young airmen in the military. He also has a good amount of experience coaching club and High School volleyball. From his research, interviews, and personal experiences he has come to the belief that coaching a sport is the purest form of professional development. He's got me convinced.

Marty's fascination with the mechanics of building and developing a staff has led him to write a book that is easy to read and simple to implement. You will learn to see things through his eyes and, in doing so, will become more adept at assembling and developing your own team. Marty's style lends itself to your being able to adopt the principles and concepts which will be most helpful to you, your team and your organization. You, of course, need to develop your own style and modus operandi, but will find it easy to pick and choose from his offerings.

At the college level we coaches direct squads as small as 8-10 (tennis, golf) or more than 100 (football). There are many ways to solve a problem and it is up to you to decide which of them best fits your particular situation and style. As you read this book, try to introduce the principles offered into your own situation to see if it will be a good fit.

Like all of his books, this one is very readable and easy to understand. As with the best coaches, Marty takes complex concepts and explains them in simple terms allowing you to grasp them early and completely. He understands that no two people are exactly alike.

Styles vary, but the goal of excellence does not. In football Vince Lombardi was a yeller while Tom Landry rarely raised his voice, yet each was a consummate organizer and won multiple Super Bowls. John Wooden appeared to be the model of decorum on the UCLA bench, while Bobby Knight freely expressed his opinions to referees and players alike. Both won NCAA championships. They shared many principles and practices, while being unique in their own ways of doing things. Organizational excellence took the squads of all four of these coaches to the top of the mountain.

Marty takes you along the journey of identifying the tasks that make up a specific role to an analysis of four key factors describing each task. These factors provide guidance on tools and processes for developing the person filling the role. The journey then continues into an analysis of the skill levels needed to perform the job and the skill levels of each individual filling the position. The gaps between the two are where the rubber meets the road and growth happens. You might think I'm making this sound too simple, but it's really Marty who has simplified the process.

I hope you have as much fun as I had with *The Professional Development Toolbox*. If you are open to constructive criticism you will see the nuggets to success that are sprinkled through the book, just waiting for you to recognize and apply. Marty's military background, professional successes, and experiences with competitive athletics; especially the way coaches achieve their goals, combine for a singular perspective that is both direct and simple to adapt. You will recognize methods you already employ and see others that you can add to your quiver of arrows.

Enjoy, learn, and become even more successful,

Bobby Bayliss
Notre Dame Men's Tennis Coach 1987-2013

Prologue

Don't skip this!

This section provides some guidance for those who aren't sure they need this book or professional development plans. Think of it as an introduction (wait – almost everyone skips over the introduction) or better yet, think of this as a preview…this section should help you determine if this book is right for you. It may also help you pitch the idea of professional development plans to your boss. But, if you're confident that you already understand the need for development planning and feel equally confident you need this book, feel free to skip ahead to Chapter 1-3, "How to use this book."

Understanding the big "why" behind professional development

I have spent more than three decades working in organizations which were trying to become more mature, more collaborative, and more effective. The one constant from the military, to higher education, to corporate America is the yearning to become better. Each and every organization I worked for sought improvement. Every good leader I worked for (either directly or from way down the chain of command) has wanted to move their organizations toward excellence.

It is their spirit of growth which encouraged me to write this book.

It is their spirit which gives me more than hope…it gives me faith that good leadership is *not* an oxymoron. Good leadership is alive and well. And where it's lacking, is not because of a deficit of desire but instead a lack of insight and knowledge.

So I wrote this book upon a foundation of faith and belief that good leadership can and will triumph. When my coauthors and I wrote

"Why Organizations Struggle So Hard to Improve So Little: Overcoming Organizational Immaturity" we diagnosed the causes of the failures which plagued most attempts. We also provided a solution that allows for overall organizational growth. A simple premise actually – based on the concept of believing in the employees – the same faith required to follow those leaders is required for them to lead their followers. The concept of using champions to make change happen will work. It has worked in the past, it works today, and it will continue to work in the future.

In "*Metrics: How To Improve Key Business Results*," I offered leaders a means of using measurements to help the organization grow and mature. Metrics is a mature behavior which many organizations are not ready for. But, I've learned that if the leader can wield this two-edged sword (metrics can help *and* hurt) with honor and loyalty, and with focus and purpose – it can become a catalyst for the very growth required to fully benefit from its power.

This next book in what is becoming a series – for in truth, each book belongs to the other –explains how leaders can build a highly functioning team. And by leaders, I mean *you.*

If you're still with me, I have to offer you another thought. A foundational belief. You can learn a lot through association. This belief is founded on my own life experiences. I learned how to hit a volleyball by learning to throw a football. I learned how to teach by learning how to write computer programs. And I learned how to write by learning how to draw. I learned to coach by learning how to be an Air Force officer.

Actually, this example may be a poor one. I'm not a hundred percent sure which came first – which was the chicken and which was the egg. Perhaps I became better at both as I learned about each. During ten years as an Enlisted (think worker bee) and then attending an intensive (and awesome) officer training program I learned the foundations of good leadership. Over the next ten years spent as an officer, spent reading, listening, experimenting, and learning I continued to sharpen my understanding of leadership and development. I also coached children, teens, and adults in sports during this timeframe. My specialty was volleyball, but I found that I could coach pretty much any sport. I took on sports for my kids which I had no fore-knowledge of and quickly realized that coaching, like being an Air Force officer – wasn't dependent on the sport, mission, or job. It was an independent skill.

There are many of these independent skills – like teaching, public speaking, writing, leading, and coaching. They are skillsets independent of the specific topic you teach, speak about, write about, lead, or coach.

I wholeheartedly believe you can learn to lead any organization by learning how to coach a sport's team. It's interesting how we regularly honor the exceptional coach and how we see winning in sports as honorable. In contrast winning in business is sometimes met with jealousy and disdain. This may be in part because it is incorrectly believed that winning in business is synonymous with greed. This is compounded by the incorrect belief that success in business is only measured by the "financial bottom line."

But when you look at a successful coach – at any level (High School, College, Semi-pro, or Professional), you simply think of a winner. Championships – or being the best – is an excellent measure of success. And since I'm trying to provide guidance to leaders of organizations it makes sense to use the sports coach as a model. I'm not in the least interested in trying to convince a sports coach that they can learn from a business leader. Of course there are some exceptional leaders that not only could qualify but who are asked to speak to teams as motivators or to provide inspiration. But this book is specifically designed to help the business leader, not the sports coach.

Bobby Bayliss, a top NCAA tennis coach, has expressed that relevance as a coach is found through making a difference in the lives of his players and helping them to excel. Interestingly he doesn't measure success by winning championships or even making super-effective teams. The development of individuals trumps winning (what most would think is the key mission of a coach). Why should it be any different for a leader in any other organization?

Do you need this book?

In my first book, "*Why Organizations Struggle So Hard to Improve So Little: Overcoming Organizational Immaturity*" (WOSSHTISL), written with Michael Langthorne and Donald Padgett, we introduced the concept of Organizational Immaturity and explained why most attempts at organizational improvement fail. Later in the book, we discussed some of the classic advanced behaviors which indicate growing maturity. A large part of the discussion centered on how to implement some of these behaviors even when the organization isn't ready for it at the enterprise level.

In my second book, "*Metrics: How to Improve Key Business Results*," I delve deeply into one of the most advanced behaviors introduced in the first book. The key to implementing these behaviors has to do with the level of implementation – at the unit, department, or organization level. Metrics is an extremely complicated and risk-filled advanced behavior which I did my best to present as straightforwardly as possible. This required that the book be substantial.

With this new book, *The Professional Development Toolbox,* focused on creating professional development plans (something I've been doing for over thirty years), the topic can be fully presented in a much smaller tome. While metrics required greater base knowledge, the creation of development plans is much simpler. This book is for anyone (managers, teachers, or coaches) wanting to create development plans for their workforce, their students, or their players. Development plans aren't only for business. They are useful for anyone who deals with complex tasks.

A question I've been asked is why I wrote a book on metrics first? I started delving deeper into the advanced organizational behaviors we introduced in WOSSHTISL with metrics because it is an incredibly hot, yet misunderstood, topic. I've witnessed too many organizations trying to force metrics across the enterprise, thinking they are some kind of 'magic bullet.' The damage "bad metrics" cause and the current trend of organizations (from large corporations all the way down to kindergartens) pushing to have metrics required me to write that one first.

I'm happy to now be able to turn my attention to professional development planning. Professional Development is where I entered the Organizational Development realm as a young Airman in the United States Air Force. I'm also happy to turn my attention to it as it carries with it none of the risks metrics does, but offers a straight forward opportunity to build excellence and achieve success. So if you think this book is for you, let's get started.

PART ONE
Laying the foundation

Chapter 1-1
Organized sports is big business

Many organizations already have some type of development plan in place (or at least in mind) for most workers. If there isn't a development plan, there is almost always a training budget. I take it as a positive sign that even when times are tough and funding for Organizational Development programs are being cut, training funds seem to survive. I believe this is because leaders and organizations intuitively know that training is required to improve skills, keep up with changes, and get the best return on their largest investment; their workforce.

While I'm pleased to see that almost every organization has some funding for, and some focus on, training, I am regularly disappointed at the lack of formality and completeness of development programs. Many times the essentials of a robust plan are missing:

1. Clear identification of what is required
2. Clear statement of the level of performance expected
3. An assessment of the current capability of workers filling a given position
4. A means of tracking training solutions

Also lacking are the synergistic benefits from having robust plans.

1. A database of organizational skills, capabilities, and solutions
2. The use and support of proper job aids where needed
3. Open and frequent conversations about individual development

So, while most organizations and their leaders speak favorably of developing their workforce, there is rarely a well-orchestrated program in place for doing so. This is why I want you to think of yourself as a coach rather than a manager. One of the first lessons I learned as a volleyball coach was that I had to plan out my practice sessions. Even if I didn't follow the plan to the letter, without a plan in hand, the practice lacked continuity and quickly became frustrating for the players and myself. What I intuitively knew was that every practice had two distinct purposes. To prepare the team for the next game and to improve each and every player's skills and knowledge of the game. I normally found myself spending the majority of the practice time on the latter.

The younger the player – the more time was spent on their development and less on game planning. Development of your team is critical to your success.

Before I go into the details on how to create professional development plans, here's a simple self-assessment to determine if you may be one of the supervisors, managers, or leaders who *need* this book. Don't worry if you turn out to be ahead of the game, this book can still be a great help in creating a robust plan for each of your workers.

If you answer yes to any of the following questions, not only will this book be of great use to you, but you truly *need* this book. Feel free to answer these questions with others in mind to determine whether this book would make a good gift.

1. Your plan is to hire workers who are already fully skilled or trained in the position you have open
2. You don't know exactly what your staff does
3. You don't know exactly what the open position requires the worker to do
4. You don't actively participate in training your workforce
5. You have never evaluated the training solution you paid for

6. You leave the selection of training solutions to the worker
7. You let the worker determine if she needs training
8. You don't know exactly what your workers are capable of
9. You think cross-training is a means of mixing up your exercise workouts
10. You only know your workers' strengths and weaknesses anecdotally

If you answered no to all ten, congratulations! You may not need this book. If you have development plans for your workers, I have to assume the methodology is as good or better than the ones you will be able to create using this book. I also assume that you have a great relationship with your workers and openly discuss their strengths, weaknesses, and development needs on a regular basis. Not only don't I mind if you decide you won't need this book...but please contact me so I can recommend you as a boss to those seeking employment. I also suggest you add "coach" to your list of experiences.

For the rest of you, who answered "yes" more often than you want to admit, this book will help you immensely. The development program you create will even be more valuable. Just following the guidance in this book promises to provide great returns for the time and resources you'll invest.

Forming a winning team

Even if your organization is over 100 years old, it helps to think about starting anew. It helps to see the organization as it would look from a blank slate.

A football team may be the best example for my purposes – it has a lot of players, the most of any major sport I can think of. It has different units – offense, defense, and special teams. Some of those units are static – like the offensive line. The makeup of some teams is very volatile, like special teams – where players matrix together to work on special projects, like kickoffs, punts, or field goals. Add to that special groupings based on the game situation (3rd and long defense, 3rd and short, 4th and 1, goal line, red zone, etc.). There are many specific roles – each with different needs in physical size and make up, but also talent and temperament.

Regardless of the team you are forming – an entire division or a department, you can use the concepts of professional development as the foundation for forming the team.

In "*Good to Great*," Jim Collins said you form a good team by "getting the right people on the bus." But there's more to it than simply getting them *on* the bus. You then have to get them in the right seats. And to finish off the analogy, if there is anyone on the bus who shouldn't be – *kick them off the bus.*

So how do you get the right people on the bus? If you try to get fully skilled and knowledgeable people to fill your team, you'll spend a ton of money on the free agency market and trades. But the way most professional teams do it (and how high school and college teams *have* to) is through drafting and recruiting. This means that you *have* to develop the players. And this fits Collins' mandate quite well. Coaches care less about current skill sets than about the player being coachable. This vague idea, being able to learn, to take direction, but also to excel, is at the heart of who you want on the bus. You are looking for three attributes in your recruits:

1. The potential to be great
2. The ability and desire to learn
3. A great attitude

Potential for greatness

This may scare some of you. It's hard enough in the interview process to identify qualified individuals with a decent attitude. I'm asking that you look even deeper into the person and determine his or her potential for greatness.

The potential to be great is critical. You don't want to hire someone who you work really hard to develop, believing he will someday obtain mediocrity. A person's resume, their vitae, their history should tell you what they already can do. Some organizations use tests – some written, some hands on – to determine if the hire can do certain tasks they've already attested to having capability in. This is a very short-sighted hiring process. You are only determining if the hire can do the tasks you need them to do…today. If the tasks change, you have no idea if they will be able to master the new requirements. You won't know if he will be able to grow with your business' changing landscape. The worker needs to help make your organization better. It's not enough to *do your job*. You want hires who will grow with your organization.

You don't want to hire someone who you work really hard to develop, believing he will someday obtain mediocrity.

Mediocrity isn't good enough. Doing the job, without the potential for improvement, isn't enough. If this seems harsh, I'm sorry, but you want the potential to excel. Throughout my work life, I've heard that "our workers are our greatest asset." The saying doesn't go, "our workers are our most expensive asset" or "the asset which costs the most." Greatest asset reflects value, not cost. But, many managers only see the bottom line involved. They are over-focused on the cost analysis. They lament that salaries account for the majority of their outlay and miss the point. They are the cynics Oscar Wilde referenced when he said they "*know the price of everything, and the value of nothing.*"

The reason the staff are the organization's greatest assets is because they have the potential for greatness. Buildings decay, equipment ages, and funds are transitory. The only asset most companies have which can move the organization into new arenas is the employee. The only asset which promises to improve with age (unless you have stock in wine) is the employee. Think about your favorite sports team. The key for success has always been a combination of scheme, process, and talent. And talent can overcome weaknesses in scheme or process. You want to hire talented people, but more importantly, they have to have the potential for greatness.

Mike Sprouse wrote in his book, "*The Greatness Gap,*" about how he consistently realized his potential for greatness in varied fields of endeavor. This potential is less a result of calculated levels of capability and more a function of attitude, perseverance, and self; self-discipline, self-esteem, and humility.

Attitude, perseverance, and self

Attitude is pretty obvious and most people understand what I mean when I say hire based on attitude. You want a team player, someone who puts "service before self" and someone who is generally upbeat and positive. Service doesn't only mean the job. It means putting others ahead of yourself. It means a selfless attitude.

Perseverance is another commonly understood trait. You want to hire someone who won't give up on the organization, on their beliefs, or on themselves. I believe these two are pretty clear.

Self though is an area that is greatly misunderstood. I find this humorous since the word should clarify the issue. It's not about leadership, it's about the worker. Potential requires self-discipline. The worker has to "*be coachable.*" She has to be *able* to change. Actually, she has to be eager to change. She has to like improving, growing, and learning.

To be valuable to an organization you have to like improving, growing and learning

---

Some managers think it's their job to instill confidence in their workers. Coaches fall into this fallacy also. They believe that they have to build up the confidence of their players – especially the ones who have a role which requires higher mental acuity. Quarterbacks, and field goal kickers easily come to mind, but also running backs who fumble too much or receivers who drop passes. You believe confidence is the major factor for any otherwise qualified individual who seems to have issues with carrying out their critical tasks. And this is probably true, but the belief that a coach has to *give* that confidence to the player is wrong. Many sports analysts looking for faults to expound upon point to the coach who doesn't leave the faltering player in the game...because they aren't given the chance to "gain confidence." Coaches have battled for ages trying to figure out how to build and maintain the confidence of their team.

Granted a coach can hurt a lesser player's confidence, but she cannot create confidence that doesn't exist. It is believed that you gain confidence by succeeding. This is oxymoronic when you think of the very successful entrepreneurs who continuously fail until they finally succeed and succeed big. It is well documented that Michael Jordan didn't make his high school's basketball team as a freshman. His confidence wasn't destroyed. He rose to the challenge. Self-confidence is born of self-esteem. Self-confidence requires that you believe in your own potential. Here is another chicken-and-egg dilemma. Do the accolades come first to create self-confidence or does self-confidence garner success and therefore applause? I believe you have to believe in yourself and then the applause will come.

Self-confidence requires that you believe in your own potential. You don't have to be great, just believe you can be.

I watch the new concept of "trophies for all" in youth sports and I cringe. False praise does not create self-confidence or improve self-esteem. Again, you can damage each with constant negativity, but because you can tear down a house doesn't mean you have the ability to build one.

A coach cannot give confidence to a player or a team. That's why they haven't found a way to do so. We are highly complex organisms which cannot be fine-tuned by someone else. There is no great manipulator, no puppet master that can make us perform as wanted. The only person who can control your thoughts, actions, and perceptions is you.

So, rather than hire talent and make plans to build up confidence and esteem – reverse your thinking. Rather than hire based on past experience and expecting to motivate – reverse your thinking. Hire for potential. Hire for those who want to grow and learn. When you hire this way you will have to then develop them, which is a lot easier and more productive than trying to motivate or create self-esteem in them.

Humility is the last factor I use to define the potential for greatness. It is the balance point for self-confidence and self-esteem. "…Conduct your affairs with humility, and you will be loved more than a giver of gifts. Humble yourself the more, the greater you are…" Sirach 3:17-18. This was the passage which provided my "ah ha" moment, a small epiphany.

When I suggest you seek out a person with humility, I don't mean false humility – like the lack of confidence. Along with a good view of self, a potential hire has to be humble. Humility means wanting to give applause more than receive it. It means not focusing on your own strengths, but instead focusing on the wonderful attributes of others. If you focus on yourself, demanding accolades you've earned…you lack humility. Instead focus on others and cherish their greatness. Find the best in others and applaud them. You want team players on your bus.

Humility requires us to realize that no matter how much we achieve, we can still improve. No matter how great you are (I'm willing to admit that you might be pretty awesome), you are truly no better than your fellow worker. You may have talents that I don't, but in turn, I have strengths that you lack. Read the unfiltered writings of Albert Einstein, one of my personal heroes and you will hear the humility in his words. He doesn't put himself above others – in spite of the brilliance he achieved.

Check any of the really great men and women through history…and the best of the best had a healthy view of themselves. Rather than demand recognition, they sought to applaud others. You want this in your hires and team members.

The ability and desire to learn

This is critical. You can't develop someone who doesn't want to improve. You can't train someone who doesn't want to learn. But you also need someone who has the ability to learn. You want to pick people with a proclivity toward the functional expertise involved. You don't want to recruit a running back who hates running the ball and only wants to tackle people. This is an important and difficult assessment to make. Both factors are needed. If you have the ability to learn but lack desire, you'll be a reluctant student. If you have the desire but lack the ability, you will be an incompetent one. The tricky part is you can't evaluate on these factors by looking at a resume or a list of certifications. In this case past experience does not predict future success. You'll have to spend some time with the potential hire and use your skills of observation.

The good news is, if the person has the right attitude, chances are these two will take care of themselves.

A great attitude

Fitting into the team's chemistry is more important than abilities or skill sets. You don't want just a good attitude. Not an attitude you hope to change to make the person a "team player." Attitude isn't something you want to develop or train. You want that as a prerequisite. Granted you have to sell them on your team and on your institution. And you do that by selling the recruit on the values, mission, vision, and goals of your organization. They have to want to be a part of your team.

Attitude may be the hardest to evaluate and the most important attribute to have. Develop tests, ask the right questions and listen carefully to the answers. If possible, provide a probation period once you think you have a good hire. Spend the time, money, and effort to get this right.

Teams have scouts and recruiters that specialize in getting the right players for the team. Elite teams at the college and professional levels learned long ago that the trick is to spend the money upfront to get the right hire. And they are also willing to cut players from the team when they realize they've made a mistake.

How to recruit

Forget the laundry list of mandatory prerequisites you normally use. Collegiate degrees in discipline X. Experience in software Y. Certifications in method Z.

There should be no mandatory requirements other than;
potential for greatness, a desire and ability to learn,
and a great attitude.

Are you ready for radical? Nothing should be mandatory. List all of these as preferred prerequisites and really mean it. All of these factors can be obtained after you hire the person. The only mandatory prerequisites should be the three attributes above: A potential for greatness, a desire and ability to learn, and a great attitude.

Which brings us to some basic foundational information required before you can recruit someone: Core organizational values, your mission, and that vision stuff. This is not a book on Organizational Development (see "*Why Organizations Struggle So Hard To Improve So Little: Overcoming Organizational Immaturity,*" ABC CLIO, 2011 for that), but you can't build a robust professional development program without people to develop. And you can't bring in the right people to develop unless you can sell them on joining your team. No matter how good your team is, no matter where you stand in the pantheon of success, no matter how much money you can offer – you have to sell them on your values, mission, vision, and goals. So, you have to know these up front.

And I don't mean a well-written, lengthy mission statement. Or a set of glossy posters depicting your organization's values. I mean you have to know them, believe in them, and sell them to the recruit. They should be a shared understanding among the whole team.

Imagine any sports team without goals, without values, and no direction. No matter the level, the team is better when it knows why it exists. When it has purpose and a vision. This is no different for a work team.

It's much better to hire based on the three criteria listed above and then train, or develop your players with the skills that they need to succeed. And of course you want them to excel, to realize their potential to be great. So you don't stop their development.

In high school and college sports, the coaches *know* they only have that talent for about 4 years and yet the good coaches never stop developing those players. Even when they're seniors and on their way "out." Why is that? Why do the good coaches keep developing players even when they know they're soon to leave the team?

There are residual benefits to developing others. You have to take advantage of these benefits and not fear losing your investment. I liken this to the marketing benefits a university gains when a graduate attains lofty stature. If your players consistently make it to the next level, your reputation as a place that develops talent grows. Along with this reputation comes a desire to join your team. Yes, you may lose your best workers periodically, but you will replace them with the best up-and-coming talent. And the network you will create will pay other benefits. This is a much preferred state over having staff who are happy with mediocrity.

---

*It's not a positive that people never leave
your organization.*

Remember, you want to recruit the eager learner, not the reluctant student. An interesting observation from sports is the best players are normally considered "students" of the game. And I'm talking even the best professional players. LeBron James is considered possibly the "best basketball player in the world today" and most sports pundits point to not only his athletic ability and size – but his skills *and* his knowledge of the game. He studies it. He knows the history. He not only practices different moves (post moves, left hand, right hand, dribbling, shooting, rebounding, boxing out, etc.) but he also studies the opposing team's defenses, offences, and the players he competes against – he knows their tendencies, strengths and weaknesses.

There is always more to learn. There is always room for improvement.

For the Armchair Quarterback: There is a lot of specialization (much like the current work environment), but there are a ton of skills required to be great at any role. From the Quarterback to the Left Guard. Wide receiver? How about the hybrid pass blocker/run blocker receiver – known as the tight end? One of those pioneers was Paul Brown, the coach of the Cleveland Browns. Brown found unique ways to use the special attributes of the tight end position especially in blocking techniques and passing schemes. In the 60's Mike Ditka was one of the first players to make the Tight End position a weapon for his team. The point is, there is always room for innovation and creativity – based on a professional development foundation! Think about it...if you expand the skill set for a position, it allows for more flexibility. Magic Johnson became the first Point-Guard-Forward-Center! LeBron is considered a Point-Forward. We are now seeing "running" quarterbacks – not just the scrambling Fran Tarkington model (which was an innovation at the time) but full-fledged weapons to run for long yardage as well as pass with accuracy. This is cross-training at its best! Of course this is true for things other than sports, like your business.

You'll need a general development plan for a given position – which all new recruits for that position will attend. But then you have special development plans for cross training opportunities depending on the potential of the player. And finally you'll have specialty training because you will have your own unique game plan, plays, and systems. This is the same for a business. No two businesses are exactly alike. Some will have a position which is an additional duty at another business. Some will have hybrids like the tight end, while others will stick to more isolated roles. There will be silos vs. full matrices.

On occasion you get really lucky and pick up a very skilled, talented player. A four or five star recruit. Even this standout will need development. Even if he is the best player on your team already, or the best in the role you picked him for, he still needs to be developed. The better he is, the better the team will be. You should want every player to obtain their greatest potential.

Imagined risks

As with any team, you run a small risk of losing these talented people once you train them. They can transfer to a different team for numerous reasons; they can become ill, or injured, or overqualified, or they may simply lose interest. They may seek another team inside or outside the organization to provide greater challenges or rewards. It's a risk, but recruiting mediocrity so you can keep a hire forever is a much worse risk.

If your hiring process makes it extremely difficult to get the right people on the bus, then change the hiring process. Don't settle because it's too hard to navigate the bureaucracy.

The fear of losing your worker because you helped her to excel has to be the worst excuse I've ever heard for not having a professional development program. Unfortunately, it's also the most common one. In essence you'd be arguing that you shouldn't help to make your people great because then they will leave for better jobs. It's hard for me to even write this with a straight face. Managers actually try to sell me on the theory that it would be better to keep their workforce mired in minimum competencies than to lose them because they become highly skilled. I am usually flabbergasted – and have no witty response. I also move on to other clients who see the light.

Your workforce is truly your greatest asset. Success is defined by how well you help these people develop, grow, and succeed. When the occasional employee moves on to a better position; in small part due to the help you've provided, this is also a good thing for you. You end up seeding your competitors and collaborators with people who have reached their potential thanks to you.

A quick side note: age does not factor into this evaluation. Many incorrectly believe that you need to hire young college graduates or wunderkinds to find the potential for greatness. I know for a fact this is faulty thinking. People grow and learn every day of their lives. Age and experience provide a whole special set of talents and potential which haven't even begun to be tapped in our youth. The potential for greatness knows no stereotypical bounds.

Late Bloomers.

Ray Kroc began McDonalds after age 52, John Pemberton created Coca-Cola at age 55, Harland Sanders used his $105 Social Security Check as a start at 65 to create the Kentucky Fried Chicken franchise, Alan Rickman (in my opinion the best Sheriff of Nottingham although most will know him as Professor Snape) got his first movie role at 46, and Julia Child didn't learn to cook until she was in her 40's. Age is just one of the stereotyped, or worse, self-imposed barriers. There are those who have achieved great things with physical limitations, monetary problems, criminal records, and addictions.

Don't manage...coach

Ok if you think all of that was kind of radical...you'll love this. If you are the CEO of a company, you should be more of a Head Coach than a manager. Who wants to be managed anyway? I don't. I don't even want to be supervised.

I want to be coached. I like to believe I am a very coachable person. I love learning new things. I love having an objective assessment of my strengths and weaknesses. I especially love it when someone cares enough to give me advice on how to improve. I'm a fiery competitor – which means I'm passionate about my sports. I'm also the same at work. I'm a team player – and I relish in my teammates' successes as much as my own. I love to help others excel and be the "best that they can be." Who wouldn't want to play with someone who makes them a better player vs. the ball hog or glory hound?

Why in the world would you hire those people? You wouldn't put them on your sports team, so why hire a selfish person for your work environment?

Nope – if you want to be a great leader – be a great leader. Head Coaches have to be great leaders. You have to be honest, you have to have integrity. You have to instill loyalty. You have to demand excellence. You have to be trusted. And your best bet at being successful – at winning tons of games and perhaps being the best team out there is in a large degree related to how well you develop your players. The same is true for a great CEO.

Every manager below the CEO is an assistant coach. Every supervisor is a special positions coach. If you have more layers of supervision than a football team has coaches – I'm willing to bet you're not flat enough.

Remember, while this book isn't going into how to start a business or be a CEO, these basic tenets are essential to being a great organization and have to be in place to have the best professional development programs possible.

You have to treat your workers, not as hired fodder which you don't care about or develop, but as members of a team. Their development is critical to the organization becoming great. Imagine a player on any unit of your football team who does *not* feel like he is part of the team. That he doesn't understand how his role fits into the goal, mission, or task at hand.

Forming any sports team, you have to make sure the players understand the ultimate goals are for the team – regardless of level or ages. The only goal can't be to "make money" or "win games." If you over simplify it in this way you fail to give a full understanding of the purpose.

In high school, athletes think and are even told by family and sadly sometimes the coach – that the purpose of playing is to have fun. Get some exercise. And maybe win some games. This love-affair with mediocrity is hurting not only our children but our country's competitive standing in the world. We now reward mediocrity and take away incentives to be great. Only the rare athlete who dreams of being a pro someday will drive herself to be great. And this is done in spite of the systems we've put in place instead of as a normal result. Granted there are some "competitive leagues" and "travel teams" but we are teaching all the non-all-stars that mediocrity is fine. Just as long as they have a good time. This viewpoint should not be sold nor bought. We have to strive for excellence in all we do. Tempered with the understanding that we're not all meant or built to be great at everything – but that doesn't mean we shouldn't work for it or strive for it.

At one of the times in my life when I needed sound guidance, my Chief Master Sargent gave me great advice. I was disenchanted with leadership and was feeling as if my hard work wasn't noticed. I was attempting a restart in my career and his advice was good, "No matter what task or job they give you, do it as well as you can and become an expert at it." This was probably the single best piece of advice I ever received. Not just about jobs and careers but about life.

In a football scenario, you have many different roles/positions. You can find out what these are from books, from watching other teams, speaking with coaches, or watching a game on TV. This is a luxury…it's a great thing to have thorough position descriptions, well-defined roles.

Are your positions as well-defined? If not, why not? It makes development for those who fill those roles much easier if the position is well-defined. Do you have position descriptions for each? Are they up-to-date?

You need thorough position descriptions. Each worker has to know what tasks are required for their position and how well they need to perform them. Are you satisfied with players who can only perform at the bare minimum? Or do you want them to be "great?" Do you want certain players to be able to act as "coaches on the field?" The more skilled the player, the more creative and innovative they can be. The more they will help improve the organization. The better team you will have. They can think on their feet and make decisions. They can make your team better.

Is this too competitive? If you think you just want to survive, that your organization shouldn't be thinking about how it can improve and be the best it can be (much less the best there is), no worries. Empty your hands and step away from this book. Don't buy this book. Go do something else. On the other hand, if you want to excel, and you want your organization to be the best it can be, then read on…we're on the same page.

Any given position has more than just skills – there are also physical expectations and personalities. A kicker needs a certain temperament. They may want to be left alone, they need to focus. They may not want a lot of cheering or motivating. They need consistency and quiet. Friendly banter may not be the best thing for a kicker. They don't need to get along with everyone all the time.

Others are natural motivators. They are passionate and intense. They will protect their house. Each role contains more than just the skills needed, but a type of attitude/personality which will help identify the best fit. There a ton of books available and tools; MBTI, DISC, etc...

Kids seem to gravitate to the roles and positions which match their personality. They go out for positions which they feel comfortable in, ones that fit their self-image.

It's neat when you see open tryouts and the coaches run everyone through some drills and then ask, "What position are you going out for?" What if you had a hiring process that was similar? Where you gave some basic personality/attitude tests followed by the question – "What position are you trying out for?" What if, instead of hiring a programmer, truck driver, or administrative assistant – you were recruiting members for your team? How would your hiring processes change? How would your attitudes about it change?

This isn't far-fetched. One of the basic benefits of having a solid professional development program is that you can *stop* trying to hire the perfect fit – especially when that "fit" has nothing to do with the team chemistry and everything to (incorrectly) do with the skill level of the worker. Instead of trying to get the fully-skilled worker at near-entry-level salaries, you can get great attitudes who want to learn and have the potential to be great! You then develop them into the roles/positions they want to try out for. You may think this is fine for a start-up company or some progressive place like Google or Dream Works...but it's feasible for any organization.

No coach would expect to get a recruit, draft choice, or rookie who can walk on the field on day one and perform all of the tasks required of the position, to the level needed. You should look for the potential to be great, a good attitude, and a willingness to learn. The head coach will assign a position coach to work with the recruit. They will find outside experts to help develop specific skills. They will team the new player with a more experienced skilled player. The job is to teach, develop, and groom that new recruit for greatness. There is no hoarding of information, selfishness to knowledge, or What's-In-It-For-Me (WIIFM) attitudes. Teams understand that what's good for the team is good for everyone and instead of WIIFM, you get WIIFMO (What's-In-It-For-My-Organization)!

The exception is if you trade for, or pick up, a free agent. Even then, you need to bring that player up to speed on your system. Note though that this will cost you much more money than bringing in and developing a new recruit. That's why this works for any size company – from a small mom-and-pop restaurant to a gigantic Industry leader.

Having a solid development program avoids the boredom that inflicts many workers. The players continue to grow, to improve, and to become better.

Why wouldn't you develop a player? If you've decided that the potential hire is the best that he will be, and no matter what you do, they are "stuck" where they are…why would you hire that person? Unless they're a top-notch expert, you have to expect them to grow.

In football, you may have to throw an ill-prepared player into the game if the guy ahead of him gets hurt or is otherwise unavailable. The same things happen in business – people get sick, take unexpected vacations, or defect. You do the best you can to prep them and then you throw them into the fire. But you don't abandon them at that point – on the contrary, you work even harder with that person to help get them up to speed…you develop him. You should continuously work with your staff to help them continuously improve.

Continuous improvement should not only be used for processes. When you hire someone who has to fill a role outside of their level of expertise – you need to work with them, discuss things in between plays, going over game film. Imagine if coaches were to do what some managers do? What if the coach only reviewed the players' performance once a year? Gave useful, meaningful feedback annually? There is no possible scenario I can come up with where a once-a-year coaching session would work for any real team.

Are you really leading your team or are you faking it?

Don't worry, if you are working *with* your staff, no one will look at it as micro-managing. Just as no player thinks his coach is micromanaging them when they provide meaningful, timely, and regular feedback or when they work with together to improve his skills. For a coach to micromanage, he'd have to run out onto the field in the middle of the play and adjust the player's stance. You can't do that. And you can't do that in business either. But you can provide developmental feedback at the end of the play or half-time, or the end of the game.

Reviewing "film" in the business world is the equivalent of reviewing results and metrics. These are your tools for feedback. Just as the player can watch game film on her own, your worker should have access to the results and metrics for her efforts. She should be able to review them on her own as well as in a team setting. "Game film metrics" don't carry with them the stigma of judgment. They avoid the Fear, Uncertainty, and Doubt (FUD) of most metrics. These metrics are used to help improve the players' performance for the betterment of the team. They give you meaningful feedback for improvement. The player can determine where she needs work, where her strengths and weaknesses are. The coach helps the player by providing an objective, experienced viewpoint. The coach's job is to help the player see things more clearly and more fully – not to belittle or berate the player. The goal is to help each and every player reach their potential for greatness.

One argument against coaching

Here is the most common argument I hear against the theory of coaching-instead-of-managing. "In coaching the ultimate goal is winning championships, but in business the goal is making money." Rather than remind you that coaches will tell you that their number one goal is helping their players become the greatest they can be...I'm going to address the second clause in the argument.

Business is *not* about making money. No more than a career is about a pay check. When your business or job becomes only a means to a positive profit-margin, it's time to find a new livelihood. I've never found a valid organizational mission statement which could be distilled to "make a lot of money." This is true for government organizations, higher education, or corporate America. I've already assigned a little reading (Albert Einstein), now take a look at Dale Carnegie, Henry Ford, George Eastman, or Steve Jobs. The purpose for your organization can't be income; the profits have to be a means to a greater end. Otherwise your organization will not last.

My simple argument is that whatever your organization's goals are – if you achieve them, you win. Same as with a sports team, the team goal is to win. And the best way to win in any environment is to develop the players so that they are the best they can be.

Chapter 1-2
The professional development plan

How it works

It's actually very simple. In each of my books (*Why Organizations Struggle So Hard To Improve So Little* and *Metrics: How to Improve Key Business Results*) I try to take normally complex issues and simplify them so they are no longer a mystery. The idea has always been to provide "do-it-yourself" tools for Organizational Development (OD).

The beauty of this book is that professional development is the easiest OD concept to simplify, because it's actually simple to begin with. You'll find that it isn't complexity that keeps us from instituting development plans. It's due to misconceptions and poor management – and even these issues are simple to overcome. But first, I need to go over how and why it works as an organizational improvement tool.

At their simplest, development plans are a tool for getting people from a deficient state – one in which the worker lacks skills, knowledge or ability; to a point where they meet the needs of the organization. Positional development (or training) plans allow managers to evaluate the abilities of personnel filling a given position, identify the gap between the current skills and the requirements of the position, then schedule training, and track progress toward eliminating the gap.

The simple idea is to have a plan for each position which becomes a template for personnel filling the position.

The plan has to have some basic elements:

1. The tasks which make up the position
2. The abilities required, including the skill levels
3. The abilities of the personnel filling the position
4. Means of tracking progress toward skill attainment

This works for any position or role. Let's look at the sports analogy.

Tasks

What are the tasks a quarterback has to fulfill? At the High School level, the tasks that make up the position are considerably less complex than at college, and exponentially simpler than at the professional level. A simple task list could include: starting the play (calling hike), securing the ball, handing the ball off to a running back, passing the ball to a receiver, or running with the ball. But of course there are other tasks and each of these tasks could be broken down into smaller components.

What abilities are required?

At what skill level? The quarterback (even at the High School level) has to be able to interpret the plays sent in from the coach. The quarterback also has to make a determination when it is necessary to throw the ball away (to avoid a loss of yardage). The quarterback has to have the ability to throw the ball, run, see down the field, and at higher levels to read the defense. Many quarterbacks find when they try to play at the collegiate level that the playbook is too hard for them to grasp or they can't "read" the defensive sets being thrown at them. There are physical and mental abilities required to do the job, and these should all be identified. I have full confidence that college recruiters and pro scouts know exactly the abilities and skills their team is seeking and how to evaluate the potential hire in those areas.

But I don't only mean physical skills. It also requires the right attitude. The part that makes this all work is that even the soft-skills, like teamwork, leadership, and positive attitudes can be defined in the terms of a task to perform.

The abilities of the players filling the position

What makes one your first string and the other the third player on the depth chart? If every player you had could perform all of the tasks required AND could do them at the highest levels, you wouldn't need a professional development plan for them. Stop expecting that to happen. It's the rarest of cases, even at the professional level. It's the times when you hear the announcer say that "yeah, he's like a coach on the field. He knows the plays as well as the coach, he gets everyone in the right positions, and he'll be a coach someday."

Tracking progress

How do you continue to assess the players' abilities and track their progress? At all levels it's important to continue to improve. The goal should be for each player to become the best he or she can. Of course you also want to win games but the best way to do that is to become the best player you can be. So the professional development plan must enable the coach to reassess his players and track their progress. In college, when you have most players for four years, it's essential that they show continual development.

The basic four components of the plan are all you need. In the chapters that follow I'll help you through the process of creating a solid plan for any position based on the tasks the position performs. But, as I've told many a client, as long as you have the four components and you are actually using the plan to communicate regularly (not annually) with your workforce, life is good.

You don't have to use the template I'll offer.

With that disclaimer in place, I would still argue that the plan has to be simple to create, to implement, and to maintain. If the plan is simple, then it becomes more likely to be used. The more straightforward and simple, the better. But it also has to be robust and complete. A useful professional development plan must be able to assist managers in helping their workforce become fully qualified to perform the tasks of a given position.

A rule of thumb we followed in the Air Force was we couldn't hold an airman accountable for performing a task (at a specified level of skill) unless we first provided training to help her achieve that level.

Why it works

These plans work where others fail because of some basic principles.

Simplicity

It's not hard and can be created by anyone. I'd like to say that I've overstated this factor, but I haven't. Simplicity is critical to making it memorable, manageable, and meaningful. The key to the plan's simplicity is the focus on tasks. We're all about doing things. Managers want to "get things done" and workers want a clear definition of what's expected. Tasks give both parties what they need.

Simplicity is the key, communication is the foundation.

Communication

If simplicity is the key, communication is the foundation. You can have the greatest plans in the world – but if you fail to communicate clearly, consistently, and regularly – you will fail. A meaningful plan requires communication between workers, managers, and subject matter experts. The plan should facilitate communication. The success of a professional development plan not only requires it, it encourages it.

Completeness

A good plan is not a partial answer. It includes everything from identifying the tasks involved to the evaluation of workers' skills and training vehicles. Tracking progress, reevaluating and helping workers achieve their potential is all part of the plan.

Of course, the real way that this plan works is because you (as Captain Piccard says) "make it so." My goal is to make it so easy for you to use it that you go against the norm and actually do so. Most managers are happy to have a documented plan – regardless of how much dust it collects. They are equally happy to have the worker ask (some actually like them to metaphorically beg) for training that the worker labors to find. A few progressive managers set aside a budget (a little begrudgingly) so that the knowledge workers can maintain their certifications.

I'm challenging you to do much, much more. My goal is to remove all of the tedium and excuses so that you can do what every good coach does with her players. My goal is for you to seriously consider developing your workers as your top priority.

Your top priority should be developing your workers.

Don't settle for getting the job done. Go much further and develop your staff to be the best at what they do. Have them sought after by others. Have their expertise requested by your collaborators and competition alike. As my old Chief Master Sargent told me – "be the best at whatever you do" – and that means as a manager, or a coach – you have to help your team become the best at whatever they do. It could be washing cars, stocking shelves, or selling computers. Whatever your current position – be the best.

Making it work (in summary)

All of the steps to developing, implementing, and maintaining a living professional development plan require honest, frequent, and meaningful communication between the worker and supervisor. It requires you to care. To care more about your team than your organization. More about your organization than yourself. It requires you to put service before self. It requires character. The actual steps are simple:

1. Create a Master Task List (MTL) for the position. All positions are made up of tasks which need to be performed. Even the most soft-skilled position can be broken down into tasks. And those tasks can be further broken down into the smallest action possible. This level of task breakdown is rarely needed. Tasks are described as actions – verb, object, and subject. Tasks can be evaluated.
2. Analyze the MTL. Each task is measured by four attributes. These attributes; frequency (of performance), criticality, complexity to perform and complexity to teach, provide insights to how to train and perform each task.
3. Determine skill-level requirements. Each task is evaluated in relation to the position to determine the level of skill required. A task may be performed by more than one position – and the level of skill required may differ based on the position.
4. Evaluate each worker's ability to perform the task. Each person who fills a position – currently or projected to do so, is evaluated for their level of ability in performing each task.
5. Identify the Gaps. The gaps between the required skills and the worker's skills equals the training required.
6. Schedule Training. Don't just plan, actually schedule the training needed to close the gaps.

7. Evaluate the effectiveness of the training by evaluating the worker's skills
   (step 4).
8. Check the gap. If not closed, try different training, until either the worker is capable or it is determined that the skill is beyond the worker's ability to grasp.

Eight truly simple steps.

What if it doesn't work?

The plan works if the manager and worker use it. Even if you find that the worker can't get it, that the work is beyond their ability to grasp, the plan will still work. You may have to find another role for the player or another team for him. If the worker is incapable of attaining the skills necessary to perform the task at the required level, management has to make a decision; how to deal with someone who cannot perform the required duties of a given position?

- Release the worker, let him go
- Retrain the worker into a new position
- Modify the position to remove the skill or reduce the level of skill required

Sometimes modification of the requirements is possible when you have more than one person filling the role and you can divide the tasks unequally between the workers. The good news is that you will no longer expect a worker who is incapable of performing a given task to do so. You will not give them a "failing grade" in performance (their inability is not due to lack of discipline, dedication or effort). The worker will not feel incompetent or persecuted. You can find a better fit for the worker's skills and talents.

That's a pretty simplistic summary. I also have a very simplistic "how to" process definition which you can use to develop, implement, and maintain a professional development plan.

So, you might ask, "if it's really that simple, why read the book?" And that would be a great question.

The only answer I can provide is that I've found, even with an enthusiastic, knowledgeable coach, few follow through and use the plan to its fullest potential. I don't know why there is such a large amount of apathy around development plans. I would hope that the development of a worker would be one of (if not *the*) most important tasks in a manager's MTL. But this is not born out through action. Perhaps you don't see the role of manager as equal to a coach. I find it hard to fathom how a coach would try to be successful without developing his players. At any and every level – professional development of a player is essential to a team's success. Even if you coach in an individual sport – like singles tennis, a coach's number one priority is to help that player perform the tasks before her at the highest levels possible. That may mean developing a better first serve. It may mean developing the ability to execute a drop shot. It may also mean focusing on her strengths and finding ways to avoid her weaknesses. If your player can't hit the ball as hard as her opponents, you, as a coach have to find a way to help her excel at the task at hand – without trying to make her do what she cannot.

Perhaps that's the simple answer to why managers don't focus on developing their staff. Perhaps they don't see themselves as coaches or their workers as part of a team. Perhaps they have no clue of what it means to "win" in their particular industry.

So, I offer the rest of this book, strategically placed between the simple introduction and the simple process example at the end, to hopefully provide the enthusiastic mentoring which you may need to actually carry out the steps in the process. It's not enough to do the tasks listed…you have to do them at the required level of performance. And that level of performance requires you to be sincerely concerned with your workers' development. It requires you, as a manager, to take responsibility for developing your workers. It requires you to want them to succeed as much, if not more than you want to succeed yourself.

That said, if you feel you don't need to read on, if you don't need help to get you through the process, feel free to jump to the end. My feelings won't be hurt. But if you decide to read the pages in between, don't worry. I've done my very best to make it simple, easy, and fun to read. At the end, I hope you earn the compliment of a worker calling you "coach."

The best compliment you can receive is for a worker to call you "coach."

Note: You may wonder why I use "development plan" instead of "training plan." I grew up with training plans and that background and experience form the basis for much of this work. Later the catch phrase became "professional development" or "development plan." All of these have an organizational viewpoint rather than the "building a knowledge base/foundation" you find in higher education, and all can be used to mean the same thing – a plan for bringing an employee from a current level of capability to a desired level. So, if you are used to the military-centric "training plan" don't worry – this will work without a problem.

Chapter 1-3
How to use this book

I wanted to make this book more of a tool for Do-It-Yourself types than a book with a lot of concepts, theories, and principles. Unfortunately, as I wrote this I realized that it's important that I provide these foundational elements and not create a process guide. Most process guides fail to perform their intended function – getting people to follow the process it defines, consistently, repeatedly, and in a standardized way. A book on concepts, theories, and principles may work well as a text book, but fails to help the practitioner implement usable tools. So, as is normally the case, I had to admit that the way it's been done for years was, and still is, the right way. But there's still room for innovation!

I decided to attempt something new. I decided to make this book as useful as possible for three different kinds of readers. You can determine which type you are.

The traditional reader

You like to read the concepts, theories and principles first. You like to get a good understanding of how and why the proposed process works. Who should perform the process, when it should be performed, and how often. You want to know about the risks and expected benefits up front, before you invest any practical effort. No problem I've got you covered. Just read from the front to the back.

The doer

You know who you are. You normally skip the instruction sheet until you get stuck. On a rare occasion you'll have the instruction sheet open when you start, but there's no reason to read through the warnings and the inventory of parts. You don't organize all of the pieces and parts, ensuring you have everything listed. Most times the only time you find out a part is missing is at the end because chances are you found a "suitable sub" before you reached the point of calling the help number or counting the parts. Chances are you had a little rework because things weren't marked as obviously as you thought they should be.

Well, actually, I don't have anything for you. I mean, the idea is that you should turn immediately to part three of this book "Practicum – Do it Yourself Development Planning. But, I can't condone you skipping the instructions and jumping into the templates. I also can't stop you. So, for those of you who want to get right to the "real work" – have at it. Of course, if you get stuck, you can go back to the corresponding chapter in part two, "Concepts, Theories, and Principles" to find any missing parts.

The learn as you go

I predict there will be a good portion of readers who prefer to read a little concept and then see how it can be applied, learn a little theory and see how it comes to life. And read up on some principles and then see how to implement them. I like this personally and wish most "how to" books would allow for this. So you can read a chapter in part two and then turn to the corresponding chapter in part three.

To accommodate any of the three types of readers I have laid the book out in three parts:

- Part One you are reading now. It has some background concepts and underpinnings which you can skim or skip. The most important thing you'll get from this part is the *why*. Why you should have development plans, why you should use them and why they will be one of the best investments you'll ever make.

- Concepts, Theory, and Principles are in Part Two. I'll try to make them entertaining. I love the way coaches develop athletes – especially in team sports, so I'll use a lot of analogies.
- Part Three is where you'll find the *how to* process steps. These are written as procedural steps wherever possible.

The trick will be connections, like in a relational database – Each item in part two will have a reference to the corresponding section in part three and vice versa. So you can start in part three if you're a doer and only want to visit the supporting concepts if needed. If you like to have a foundational understanding before you delve into the procedural steps, read the chapter in part two and then jump to the corresponding chapter in part three.

The goal is to help you create a professional development plan for any person or position in your organization. I want to help you to succeed at this task and to reap the benefits along the way. This book is my way of doing that.

Regardless of which method you choose to use, I suggest that you select a position to create a professional development plan for and build it as you step through this book. You will not only learn the process better, you'll also finish the book with your first complete development plan in hand.

PART TWO
Concepts, Theories, and Principles

Chapter 2-1
The Master Task Listing (MTL)

Evaluating

In part one I offered a bit about how to assess the abilities of a potential hire – so you can decide who you want on your team. While the three criteria; Potential for Greatness, Ability and Willingness to Learn, and a Great Attitude would be categorized under "soft-skills" – there are other, more concrete skills to assess. These skills shouldn't be used to pick your hires, but they are essential to developing your staff. They are also critical in communicating what the job entails and helping the candidate to choose the right job. When you evaluate the needs of the position you will need to be very concrete and specific.

Before you recruit for a position, you need to understand what goes into the position. Before you can help someone become great at a given position, you need to evaluate the requirements for that position.

Once you have a clear definition of what goes into the position, you can then determine how well the players filling those roles are doing. Do you have a player who is raw *or* one who will probably be playing in the pros on Sundays?

A habit I've come to rely on after many years in the Air Force, is to start at the beginning. This works especially well with creating professional development plans.

The beginning for a professional development plan is the Master task Listing (MTL). This list captures the tasks that make up the position. This is the proper starting point because the MTL is the foundation for the professional development plan. The MTL is a comprehensive list of tasks which define a position. It's the listing of all tasks that are accomplished by the person filling the position. It will be used to identify the minimum job tasks that, when trained, makes a person qualified to do their job. The basis of a good development plan is that all training is based on identified requirements and that all requirements are based on actual tasks. While sources of training may, and frequently do change, the requirement for the training usually does not. The MTL is a listing of the major tasks involved in filling a specific position.

While I have chosen to use football as the primary sports analogy for this book – I have to admit that I have much more experience coaching volleyball. I have coached youth (13 year olds) all the way up to adults. When I had my first opportunity to coach at the high school level, one of my first meetings with the team included the distribution of descriptions for the positions we'd be using. If you are only a casual observer of the sport, you may not realize the various positions. The Ace Hitter (also known as Power or Left Side), Middle Blocker, Opposite, Setter, Defensive Specialist and recently the Libero. Don't worry, I'm not going to give you a primer on volleyball, but I want to point out that even in volleyball, a definitely less complicated sport than football – or probably your organization, there are specialized positions. The way I described each of these positions were twofold; the attitudes which fit best and the tasks the position would perform. This is the same for any sport and any team. You can take the requirements for any role and break it down into the tasks required to perform the job as well as the personality traits best suited for it.

In sports this may differ based on the level – high school, college, or professional. As a high school wide receiver (back to football) – the task list you are expected to perform may not include blocking. It may also not include the ability to make certain types of catches or run certain routes. And it likely won't include reading complex defenses and making "hot reads." Depending on the offensive system your coach is using, you may have different tasks and definitely different ways of performing those tasks. While the overall list of tasks a wide receiver performs may be the same at each level and across systems, *how* the tasks are performed can be taught differently. This is one of the places where innovation and creativity comes in. You can identify new tasks, matrix tasks across roles, and come up with new ways to perform the same tasks.

Regardless of the role you want to define – there will be a set of tasks to be performed. The bottom line hasn't changed or moved.

Every role is made up of tasks which can be evaluated for how well they are performed.

Let's look at how to develop the MTL.

The first prerequisite for developing the MTL is to select a position to analyze.

Why tasks?

Normally you'll see a list of skills and knowledge items filling development plans. Things like "knowledge of Unix operating systems," or "technical writing skills," or "project management skills." The problem is that these are at best ambiguous and at worst impossible to evaluate.

The reason you require certain skill sets and knowledge is for your workforce to perform the job. Performing the job breaks down into performing duties. And from duties you easily move to tasks. The most common argument against a totally task-centric plan involves soft-skills, so let's use a totally soft-skill position for your first example.

General Manager

The job can be broken down into duties: Supervise middle managers, create & maintain department budgets, communicate effectively with organizational leadership, and perform strategic planning. These duties are a bit vague, so you look a little deeper at the high level tasks that go into carrying them out. Rather than breakdown all of them I'll use one of the softest, "Supervise Middle Managers" as an example.

"Supervise middle managers" breaks down into; evaluate performance, set performance goals, create professional development plans, identify strengths and weaknesses and provide coaching. These are getting clearer – each can be used as-is to create a development plan. But you can go further if you like. "Evaluate performance" can be broken down into:

- Identify tasks
- Identify levels of performance possible for the tasks
- Observe performance of the tasks (or use another means of collecting information on the performance)
- Compare the performance against the expected level of performance

This all might seem obvious – that all ambiguous skills and knowledge items can be broken down into clearly stated tasks. I fully agree. I believe it *is* obvious. I also believe it is a critical step which is frequently overlooked.

All soft skills can be broken down into measurable tasks.
Get to the task level.

All soft skills can be broken down into measurable tasks. And that's the simplest secret to creating professional development plans that work. Get to the task level. Go as far down as necessary to allow you to evaluate the ability of the worker to perform the task.

So, where do you get the list of tasks from? Well, if you know what the job entails – what tasks make up a given job, you have the list of tasks you need for filling the Master Task List. I have rarely found this list already in existence. Do a quick check for yourself. Review the position you are using as your sample. Do you already have a Master Task List for it?

> If you are a coach this book should be very useful for you too. Do you have a list of tasks which go into each position? It's a great gift to share with your players. Back to my first high school volleyball team. I gave out position descriptions to all of the players. It didn't matter if the player was a returning starter, I wanted them all to know what went into each position. I knew I was going to have to move some players into different positions than what they had played in the past. I also wanted every player to know what her particular position entailed. This was the best thing I did as a first-year head coach. Discussing the tasks, being able to show each player the full gamut of tasks which went into the position helped show the players what was expected. I didn't even talk about the level of performance I wanted. It was enough to itemize the things that each player would have to do so that we could function as a cohesive team.

Every position should have a clear and complete list of tasks that make up the role. This *can* be done. This *should* be done. Ok, really, if you want to develop your team and move the team to be the best they can be – this *must* be done.

---

*Every position must have a clear and complete list of tasks
that make up the role.*

Thanks to the US military

The US Military, by its nature, has to excel at developing its personnel. It takes young men and women with no experience and prepares them for the epitome of teamwork. I spent twenty years in the US Air Force and every year my development was an integral part of my job. From entering the service as a young man with no idea of military customs and courtesies, to obtaining college degrees, and finally completing officer training school – development was an essential part of the day-to-day expectations.

No matter what the job or level of responsibility, the Air Force taught you how to perform it at the highest levels. This included everything from entry level positions to fighter pilots. The one constant in all of the development systems throughout the Air Force was the use of Master Task Listings.

In the Military's practical simplicity, it effectively side-stepped the issue which I now find at all levels of education. "How do you determine the effectiveness of education?" In other words, how can you determine what has been learned? This need for educators to measure their effectiveness has spilled over into the way businesses look at professional development.

This behavior stands out when you look at job descriptions. Peppered throughout, you'll find allusions to the applicant needing to have "an understanding" of a particular software or equipment. Others want "knowledge of…" or "considerable knowledge of…" or "experience in…" The simple problem is how to measure "understanding?" These are all very fuzzy phrases.

The normal solution, one used by most educational institutions, is to provide a test. But this is a notoriously poor indicator of actual attainment of knowledge. You can ace a test and still not actually "learn" the material – either by cramming or by getting the answers right, but having no idea how to apply the information.

The evaluation of the training is fully dependent
on the ability to apply the knowledge.

That's the key to the military's methodology. The evaluation of the training is fully dependent on the ability to apply the knowledge. *Application* of the knowledge is what matters. Not only is it easier to evaluate – it's a better measurement of success. Rather than test if a student can recite the periodic table or Plato's theories on the Republic – have the student demonstrate comprehension through the application of the principles. To achieve this, you use tasks.

Tasks are verb driven, measurable, things to get done.

Tasks are verb driven, measurable, things to get done. By driving everything to tasks, you can easily evaluate performance – which is what performance evaluations are supposed to be all about. By basing everything on tasks, the development plan becomes a tool for evaluating performance as well as providing training. This should (and does) make common sense. Your professional development plan should prepare you to perform on the job.

Let's look at how this works.

Simple tasks

Simple tasks are tasks where little to no knowledge is necessary to perform it. I could use any task – like walking a dog or pouring a bowl of cereal, but I'm going to keep to the sports theme throughout. An example of a "simple" task would be "get into a two point stance." I was going to use "hike the ball" – but there are actually more variables involved, making it not as simple. Is it a long snap (to a punter) or a shotgun snap or a snap to the quarterback under center? It has to have the proper height for the quarterback based on his distance from the Center and it has to have the right velocity. Nope…hiking a football isn't very simple. So instead let's look at assuming a two-point stance. In this case it helps to understand the importance of balance and where to be looking – but all-in-all you *could* consider this task "simple." There isn't a lot of background knowledge or supporting concepts required to perform this task.

But what if it is a bit more complex? What if a certain amount of knowledge is required? Like, well, hiking the ball?

More complex tasks

More complex tasks can be ones in which there is significant knowledge needed to do a task – like "analyze." The Center on a football team has a very complex job – along with proper blocking assignments, he must also snap the ball properly (height, speed, spin, distance) while reading the defense. The Center must also get the snap count correct – it's usually a mess when the Center snaps the ball at the wrong time; too early it may lead to a turnover, too late and it will result in a penalty. Many times the knowledge-based item supports more than one task. In this case, the snap starts the play and depending on the call, the snap has to be different. Teaching how to perform the task in this case actually includes performing the task in multiple ways.

This does not preclude providing base or background knowledge. If the workers need supporting knowledge to perform a task, this will be included in the training for the task– but the key is that the training is not for the purpose of *obtaining* knowledge – the goal of any training is to perform a task. The purpose is to make it so the Center can do all of the tasks required to perform the role. The knowledge is only a conduit to performing the task.

The goal of any training is to successfully perform a task.

Football is a great scenario to work under because any Monday Armchair Quarterback (spelled f-a-n) can tell you that all the supporting knowledge and concepts don't matter if you can't perform the task properly on game day. It's great to have an understanding of the game – you'll never hear that a player was too smart or too knowledgeable. But, no matter how "smart" the player is, if he can't perform the task, he won't get on the field.

The old adage makes a lot of common sense – those who can - do, those who can't (but understand the concepts) - teach. I've tested this multiple times over the years and for every knowledge-based item, there is a task being performed – a task which matters.

Let's look at a business world example. Let's say the job requires that you develop or manage metrics. I've seen requirements written such as "have a working knowledge of Microsoft Excel ©" (or insert whatever software tool you use regularly). The tasks, including; collecting data, categorizing data, analyzing data, building measures, building information, and reporting metrics, all depend on the ability to carry out these tasks within a given tool-set. You may argue that the more you know about the tool, the better it makes you and this is absolutely true. The more you know about the tools, the better you *can* perform the tasks. You can be more efficient or effective if you are an expert at the tools you will use to perform them. This is again, common sense, but for some people common sense isn't all that common.

The more you know – about a tool, about theory or underlying prin- ciples – the better you'll be able to perform the task. But, the *goal* is still the task, not the knowledge. The knowledge is an enabler for performing a task or a group of tasks.

I've found many examples of non-tasks in position descriptions and consequently in development plans, like "understand Microsoft Word ©, SPSS © tool knowledge, or Biometric calibration."

These are not tasks.

Because they are not tasks, they are hard to train or evaluate. Every pure knowledge item has a driving task associated with it. Other- wise, you'd pay your workers for sitting all day and thinking. Even customer service technicians – who you pay to be knowledgeable, are task driven. You don't pay them to "know *how* to solve prob- lems." You pay them to actually solve them (or help customers solve them).

You don't want your Center to know how to read a defense, you want him to actually do it and communicate this information to the other linemen. You don't pay head coaches to "understand the play- ers." You pay them to lead the players, to make decisions; who plays when, when to call time outs and to develop offensive and de- fensive systems. Or simply to "build a winning program." In the case of specific skills coaches, you pay them to teach those skills to play- ers – not to simply have knowledge. The knowledge component is a necessity to do something well, but you *pay* for results. You expect your workers to produce.

Complex tasks

Complex tasks require deep knowledge to perform – like "innovate" or "create"). The key here is that sometimes tasks are complex

enough that they disguise knowledge-based items as the end versus the task behind them. Programmers are a good example. One
of the best programmer jobs I have seen, at least best paying, was
for a COBOL programmer. COBOL was one of the original programming languages for the large main-frame systems first used in massive computer systems. But, with the personal computer came many
other, powerful languages like Forth, C, and my favorite Pascal. But,
the COBOL systems were so massive that it was more economical
to hire programmers to maintain these systems than to rewrite the
software. Also it was risky to rewrite it all when you *knew* that the
current version worked properly.

Even these highly knowledge-based jobs broke down into tasks.
Maintaining a COBOL system is made up of tasks. Reading a defense and making an audible into the proper play requires
knowledge – but that knowledge is necessary to make a read (task),
communicate that change to the team via an audible (task) and then
carrying out that call (task). When you evaluate the quarterback's
performance, you review the read, the call and the results. If they
don't make the right calls, if they perform the task poorly, you *then*
look into any deficiencies in knowledge. What you put into the MTL
is the task, not the supporting knowledge – even if it's required.

Supporting knowledge is important,
but it's not what you evaluate against.

Building your Master Task Listing

Finding tasks

When you look at the positions on the football team, you have the
benefit of years of public information on what goes into each role.
There are of course jobs where the "rules of the game" are not as

clear and not as available. Technology jobs are a good example because they change (seemingly) overnight, every night. Unlike the
COBOL programmer, these software and hardware systems are
changing frequently. As the saying goes – the only constant in technology is change. So, if you want to find out the tasks which go into
performing the role of Quarterback, Center, Right Guard, Tackle,
Running Back, Wide Receiver, Slot Receiver, or any other position,
you can find a lot of information. Although there are a multitude of
offensive positions, defensive positions, and special teams' roles –
the tasks which make them up are well defined and documented.

How I wish all jobs had the tasks as well defined.

Besides the ease in creating positional development plans due to
the availability of this information, perhaps a more valuable benefit
is the ability of the coach to be creative and innovate. The more
well-defined the tasks which make up a position or role are, the easier it is to innovate. Every year coaches find twists and tweaks in a
system that is supposed to have been played out. There aren't supposed to be any new ideas possible...but each year someone
comes up with something new. This is because of the wealth of task
definitions.

If you agree that your job is to coach (versus manage), you need to
know the positions and roles of your team as well as a football
coach knows his.

So, you need to find the tasks that make up the job. You'll do that by
reviewing existing documentation like job descriptions, job positions,
performance evaluations, and process definitions. When you've ex-
hausted the research sources you can then ask the workers and supervisors to provide their inputs from experience. Make sure you de-
lineate between what is required and what tasks are part of a wish
list.

You'll find if you ask what tasks make up a position that a good portion of the answers you get are what currently goes into the job. You'll also find a set of tasks which are more of a wish list. A list of tasks which could and maybe should be included in the position, but at the given time are not. Ensure you clearly identify the difference. Both can be in the plan, but it is important to denote which are *required* to get the job done.

Task breakdowns

You may find that the tasks you've identified are at too high of a level to evaluate. The litmus test for determining the right level is to ask (and answer) the question, "can you evaluate the task?" What I mean by evaluate is the ability to determine a few factors about the task:

1. How frequently is the task performed?
2. How important is it to get it right the first time?
3. How complex is the task (to perform)?
4. How complex is it to teach the task?
5. How well does the task need to be performed?
6. How well do the workers currently perform the task?

The good news is, if you find that a task is at too high a level, you can do a task breakdown. You can break down tasks whenever you need to – and, more good news, there is no penalty for leaving a task at too high a level.

As I stated earlier, the military would do task breakdowns until you got to the lowest possible level. This will be overkill for the majority of you. But, the use of task breakdowns is a valuable tool. When you look at your tasks, they should be of a detailed enough level that you can clearly tell what is to be done and how well you have to do it (after you add the performance evaluation step). If it's not, you'll have to break it down into smaller, more manageable tasks.

Task Breakdowns aren't only useful for evaluating, they are also useful for training.

When I teach hitting to middle hitters (Volleyball), I break the task down into subtasks:

1. Hitting the quick middle set
    a. The Approach
    b. The Jump
    c. The Turn
    d. Timing
    e. The Swing

Hitting in the middle is far different than hitting on the left side, the right side, or from the back row. As a coach, I know this, and have to teach each of the tasks differently. While a new player may think they are all the same, if I try to teach the task without breaking it down – that same player will make it painfully clear if I don't explain it in enough detail. If I leave out any of the above subtasks, the new player will not execute the task properly. So the best way to determine the level of detail for the task breakdown is to have an experienced person (expert, coach, or trainer) work closely with someone who is new to the task. This allows for the trainee to help the expert ensure that she fully explains the tasks.

Good coaches do this without thinking about it. When they teach a task they break it down and work with the player to develop the muscle memory and habits necessary to perform the task at the level needed. While the coach may not think about this...it's an essential teaching tool which she uses all the time. I use the qualifier *good* because I've seen a lot of (bad) coaches who don't break down tasks to help their players "get it." Instead they yell a little louder, "hit it harder" or "you've got to block him" or worse yet, "you can't throw that ball there!" None of these admonitions help the worker perform the task better. They don't even make the player feel better. Instead these remarks only make it painfully clear to the player that he is failing to do it right, with no clear guidance on how to correct the error.

Managers fall into the same trap, although it is rare that they invest enough emotion into the performance of a specific task to actually yell. But, admonitions of "faster," "with less errors," or "with more attention to detail" can be heard in the halls – albeit just above a whisper.

Good coaches instead inform the player of how to correct their performance of the task. Good coaches realize that the player already knows they did the task wrong (the consequences are usually (and thankfully) immediate and clear. The job of the coach is to help the player perform the task correctly, and then at a level equal to her potential.

Managers should have the same attitude about mistakes. They are an opportunity to help the worker learn to perform the task correctly and later to perform it at a high level. It's ridiculous how many managers don't see this as part of their job. It may be more ridiculous that it's not included in his job description.

It's less disheartening, but still a bit saddening, that many managers don't know the tasks well enough to give advice on what is being done incorrectly or how to fix it.

Logical groupings for tasks

Many times the tasks in the MTL can be grouped under a larger heading. This makes it easier to understand the relationship of the task to other tasks. It also just feels right. Rather than have an alphabetical or random listing of the tasks involved, it is comforting to see the tasks grouped in a logical set.

One way to look at these groupings is to consider them processes or procedures. A process is basically a group of tasks strung together in a sequence which when done properly results in a "job." Groupings of tasks will help you define your processes and document your procedures. They also help you with breaking down the MTL into trainable tasks. It is very useful to group the tasks you've identified as components of the position.

I'd like to tell you this is a prescriptive activity and that you can follow a set of rules or complete a template. But this may be more an art than a science. If you can group them into process sub steps – you're good to go. But if not, groupings will require that you have an understanding of the job you're analyzing.

Did I fail to mention that identifying all of the tasks that comprise a role constitutes a thorough job analysis? Sorry. But I know I mentioned that there were many beneficial byproducts from any Organizational Development (OD) work you undertake. And creating professional development plans is definitely one of the best OD activities you can perform.

The groupings you pick (outside of a process list) won't matter. What I mean is it won't matter if you get the groupings "wrong." There really isn't a right or wrong. Of course you could come up with groupings that aren't the best, but that's ok. The important thing is to group them so that you can make it a little easier to build your development plan.

So, take the time to look for logical groupings. It will make everything easier. And you may just end up with some process definitions to boot. When you're done you should have a fairly comprehensive list of tasks which go into defining the position. Remember, you don't have to have perfection out of the gate. You can always add to the list later, as you find tasks you missed or as the position grows or changes.

Short version

Tasks are the key. And so let's clearly state the tasks for this step in the development planning process.

1. Collect existing documentation which may have clues to the tasks required for performing a given job
   a. Position Descriptions
   b. Job Description
   c. Job Posting
   d. Task breakdown
   e. Occupational Studies (role descriptions for similar positions)
   f. Performance Evaluations
   g. Resumes
2. Mine documentation for tasks
   a. Look for the obvious verb-based tasks
   b. Look for the hidden tasks (disguised as skills, knowledge, expertise or "experience in")
   c. Break out compound tasks (look for multiple verbs in a sentence and conjunctions such as "or," "and")
3. Review tasks with manager and current work staff
   a. Confirm the tasks you've identified
   b. Ask for tasks you missed
   c. Take your best guess at the tasks involved
   d. For tasks you have which are still complex, ask for clarification
      i. Ask why the task is being done (to uncover other tasks)
      ii. Determine the expected end results (not just the process to reach it)
      iii. Breakdown the task until you get to a task simple enough for an "outsider" to understand
4. Group tasks logically

For the practicum on how to create a MTL, go to Chapter 3-1.

Chapter 2-2
Define Training Requirements

Task attributes

Now that you have a list of tasks, you know what the job is composed of. You now need to analyze the tasks to determine some important factors – how well the tasks need to be performed, how difficult it is to perform the task, if the tasks require training, and what is the best way to go about developing the worker's skills to perform the tasks. These attributes provide a more thorough understanding of what goes into the job. This in itself will be of great value.

The final goal is to create a plan which can be used to help employees perform the job at the required level. There are three basic questions you can ask about each task to identify their attributes.

1. Is training required?
2. If so, what type of training is best?
3. In either case, are tools/instruments called for?

Does performing the task require training?

This may seem like an obvious question – or an unnecessary one. But, just because the task exists, it doesn't mean the task is complex enough to require training. Perhaps the steps in the process only require that you perform them in a specified order, at a specified time. Let's say the task is *deliver interoffice mail*. This task may only require a short instruction sheet:

1. Collect mail from mailroom
2. Organize Mail
    a. Identify recipient

            i. If the recipient is unknown or not on the distri-
               bution list, return the item to the mailroom
      b. Identify location
      c. Group mail by recipient, then by location
  3. Deliver Mail

Of course, the process can be more complex – what do you do about an employee who is out of the office for an extended period of time? Are there any time-sensitive items that should go to the employee's alternate/supervisor in her absence? Are there any protocols which should be followed (security or safety related?). But all in all, you can see that just because a task is identified it doesn't mean that task will require training to perform.

Even so, as a coach, there are very few tasks I can think of that don't require some amount of training. I am not considering if the player already has the skills necessary to perform the task adequately. That will come later. The key is to determine if the task, if unknown, would require training. Each job, and each task within the job has to be analyzed to determine if it requires training.

If the task requires training, what type of training is best?

Training vehicles have improved steadily over the years. Computer-based-instruction seemed to arrive at about the same time as the computer. Now there is web-based training. Two examples are Lynda.com for software and ABCMouse.com for preschoolers. There is also online training, and webinars. Will self-paced, computer-based-training work? Will a formal classroom be required? Is On-The-Job training the best method? One-on-one tutoring, self-paced training, small-group training, and of course the classic classroom training. There are ½ day, full day, and even week long seminars. Colleges and Universities are experimenting with many different methods of training. There are enough variations of training that you can pick and choose which work best for the task, for your environment and situation, and for the student.

I'll leave it to you to determine the best fit for your particular environment, situation and personality. But each task also dictates the best training method for itself. By analyzing the task attributes you can objectively determine the best means of gaining the knowledge necessary to perform each task.

What tools/instruments are called for?

Even if training is not required, tools or instruments may be useful. In the example of mail delivery, the detailed instructions offered would be very useful. In other cases a simple checklist, job aid (usually a visual aid), or a quality check may be called for. Guidebooks, workbooks, and manuals fit under this heading.

Video has become a powerful tool. When I'm trying to teach a skill to my volleyball team (passing, serve receive, serving, defensive digging, setting, hitting, etc.) I find it useful to investigate new ways to communicate. Advances in technology have helped greatly in providing new ways to get a point across. Video especially has been a useful tool for teaching skills. Not only by showing proper techniques of world class players, but also by showing the player her own tendencies, strengths and weaknesses. Football teams have used video (film) for ages, but now even the smallest club or high school team can take their own video and use it to improve skills.

So, not only do you need to know if the task requires training, but what form of training would be best and finally what tools or instruments might assist in performing the task.

So how to best answer the three key questions?

These questions can all be answered through the analysis of four attributes; Frequency, Criticality, Complexity to Perform and Complexity to Learn. For each value, a simple evaluation of "low," "medium," or "high" can be used. Since there are four factors, with three different evaluative values, the permutations are considerable (81 to be exact) so I won't list them all. Instead I'll share with you the rules for each. These can be programmed into an application (if you'd like a spreadsheet programmed for this purpose you can download a free copy at my website, mkknowlegebuilders.com).

When you evaluate the tasks as either low (L), medium (M), or high (H), the judgment will be made very subjectively. This is both a weakness and a strength of the system. Because it's a best guess by you, the evaluator – it requires some amount of intimacy with the task. You have to understand the task – how it's done, when it needs to be done, how often it needs to be done, how important it is to get it right the first time, and how complex the task is. The knowledge required to make a fair (and accurate) assessment requires an evaluator who not only has done the task, but has mastered it.

So it may not be the supervisor, manager, or even the current worker who should conduct the evaluation. You may need to enlist a subject matter expert.

Even then, you will find variance since the qualifiers (low, medium, and high) are non-scientific. The reason this is acceptable, the reason it works, is that it's a tool. It's part of the process. While you want the evaluation to be as accurate as possible, if you miss the mark and choose low when you should have chosen high, medium instead of low, high instead of medium, it doesn't really matter. Because there are checks and balances throughout the system I will share with you.

A quick note: While sports analogies work well for this book, I wanted to also point out that this book will work great for a sports team. If you are a coach (or parent) you can use this book for developing your players.

So take your best shot – because it's always worth trying to do it right the first time. And if you miss don't stress out, you'll have opportunities to do better. For now, let's just go over the attributes and how they can be judged.

Frequency of performance
The first evaluation is the easiest, how frequently is the task performed by a given position, or by a given person in the role. The frequency with which a task is performed helps you answer the key questions; is training required? If so, what type? And what tools, if any, are required?

Tasks which are performed on a high frequency basis (daily for example), don't require many tools/instruments since the employee will quickly get into a routine and get to know the task very well. Using even the simple task of mail delivery – if the mail is delivered daily, the employee will quickly get to know the locations, names, and best routes to traverse to be the most efficient and effective. But if the mail is delivered only once each month, the employee may well forget much of the information that is necessary to be a high performer.

I recently turned over a daily task to a co-worker. The sharing of the workload was the right thing to do and I provided a thorough set of instructions to go with the responsibility. I also made macros so that the task was simpler and it could be done more efficiently. After a few months my coworker didn't need the instructions. She had it down pat. But, whenever she was off for the day, the task reverted back to me and I ended up needing those thorough instructions because I hadn't done it for months!

So, when thinking of the frequency, check if the position you are analyzing does the task as the primary or as the backup.

In sports, almost all tasks are performed frequently. Plays, especially special plays, are much less frequent. For the plays your team runs every game, no special memory tools are necessary.

A task which is performed infrequently may benefit from tools/instruments and may even need recurring training.

Plays that you save for special occasions (like a fake field goal) you may want to have some tools for remembering the particulars. You'll definitely want to spend more time practicing it so that when you decide to run it your team will do so effectively.

Let's look at the three point scale you'll use for evaluating each task – Low, Medium, or High. Each is relative but a simple guideline for frequency I use is:

- H(igh) = if you do the task daily
- M(edium) = if you do the task weekly
- L(ow) = if you do the task less frequently than weekly

Not to complicate matters, but these ratings are subjective. You could also go with:

- H = Daily – to – more than once a week
- M = once a week to monthly
- L = less than once a month

If you are discussing a play, high may mean that you run the play every game, medium once every other game, and low may be a play that you run only once a season. In volleyball, high frequency may be the play you run five or more times a game, medium a play your run a few times a game, and low may be a play that you run only once a game. Frequency, like all of the four factors, is relative.

For most jobs, frequency is usually based on days, weeks, and months. Depending on the task and the position, you may easily say that monthly is low and medium has to be more frequent than monthly. The analysis will result in recommendations based on the assessments you give for each, but you can of course modify the results based on your experience and needs. If the analysis shows that you don't need a job aid, but you want one, or believe one will be beneficial, you can and should develop one. For some of us (which I admit I fit this description) this will cause some anxiety – and for those, I suggest you modify the scale so that the analysis suggests what you intuitively know is right. If you need the task to be low frequency, adjust your scale accordingly. The MTL and its analysis are guidelines to help you work through the first steps in the creation of the development plan.

The work you will perform evaluating each task will reap many benefits. As with the most precious things in life, it's not the end that matters, but the journey. That may sound like a familiar platitude, but in this case it is very accurate. Throughout the process of creating a development plan you will learn about the job, the workers filling the tasks, and yourself.

While frequency speaks more to timing for the training and tools to use, the next two factors speak more to *if* training is required.

Complexity to perform
While the first attribute focuses on how to train and perform the task, the complexity attributes analyze if you *should* train. Complexity to perform is an analysis of how complicated the task is. It's not always

correct to say "how hard" it is to perform because an easy task, when combined with other easy tasks may become complicated due to the numerous choices and the criteria for making those choices. Conversely a hard task, like finding a needle in a hay stack may not be complex, just difficult. So look at the number of steps involved and the complexity of doing the task. In the end you can ask yourself if training would help you or your employee perform the task properly. Or if training would help elevate performance to the required level.

- H(igh) = Extremely complex – lots of steps, a complicated process
- M(edium) = complex – not as tough as high, but not simple either
- L(ow) = Rather simple actually

Another helpful way to look at it is; how difficult is it to explain? If you were teaching someone how to run a particular pass route, is it as easy as drawing a diagram in the sand or will you need more detailed visual aids? While "how to run a route" may be lower complexity, if you add in the task of determining the defense so you know when and if you should break off the route, it becomes much more complex.

- H= Extremely difficult to explain
- M= Difficult to explain
- L = Easy to explain

Complexity to learn
Complexity to learn is the most abstract of the four attributes and may be the most difficult to assess – especially if you have never taught the task. You have to evaluate the amount of effort it would take to pick up the task. Do you need special equipment? Do you need complicated scenarios? Would it require some base knowledge, theory or principles? If the task is complex to learn,

chances are it's a complex task. Again, finding a Subject Matter Expert (SME) will help. In this case you may want to find an SME who teaches the task for a living. The funny thing about that is that if the SME is an instructor, it should be easy for her to assess the complexity to teach the task. Is the task included in the program? How much time is spent teaching the particular task? If you have an in-house expert she can be used as your SME.

Here is one possible way to evaluate the complexity to learn attribute.

- High = Requires background info, a lot of time and effort
- Medium = Requires some info, and a decent amount of time/effort
- Low = Easy to learn, can teach yourself in less than an hour

You could once again use the difference between a task on the playing field and a play that you run. It should be obvious that a play is made up of multiple tasks, performed by different players simultaneously...which makes plays much more complex. But, let's look at a task instead. How about performing a pass rush?

If you watch Justin Tuck, a defensive lineman for the NY Giants (and a former Notre Dame Irish standout), you'll see that there are multiple techniques he uses to rush the quarterback. The task is simple. Get past the offensive lineman and get to the quarterback before he releases the ball. To an armchair quarterback, it may seem simple. If you're faster, stronger, and or bigger than the offensive lineman, you should be able to effectively perform the task. Of course it's not that simple – although physical abilities do make a difference.

What play is the opponent running? What technique is the offensive lineman using against you? Are you being double teamed? Are they running plays away from you or toward you? Selecting the correct move at the right time becomes much more complicated. So, if you break the task down to a small enough level, it may not be complex, but if you look at all of the variables and situations involved in actually implementing the task, it may become complex enough to require training.

Here's another time when a task breakdown is useful.

If I were to teach you to play chess, at a specified level of performance, let's say better than average club player, the task would be complex to teach. I realize I have little to no chance of convincing anyone that chess should be classified as a sport. I'll live with that, but I feel confident that chess is complicated enough of a game and because it can include instructors, coaches, matches, and big time tournaments − it will work well for my analogies. Let's break that large task down into some simple subtasks though.

1. How to set up the board
2. How to move the pieces
3. How to play the opening
4. How to play the middle game
5. How to play the end game
6. How to analyze a position

Notice I didn't list any supporting knowledge. There are some basic items that need to be understood to accomplish the above tasks at the level identified.

1. Names of the pieces
2. Relative values of the pieces
3. Rules
4. Definitions of key terms
   a. Check
   b. Checkmate
   c. En Passant

       d. Center
       e. Ranks and Files
       f. Diagonals
       g. En Prise
       h. Passed Pawn, Doubled Pawns, Isolated Pawns
       i. Pawn promotion

5. Concepts (tactics)
       a. Discovered attack
       b. Double attack
       c. Skewers and Pins
       d. Combinations

6. Concepts (strategies)
       a. Pawn weaknesses
       b. Positional considerations
       c. Control of the center
       d. Opposition

There's a lot more but that should suffice to show the difference between the specific tasks and the knowledge required. Along with the knowledge items, the player would have to master, to a required degree, the concepts offered so that he can perform the tasks at the needed level.

This is a very important point. Getting someone to perform a task is only part of the objective. You have to identify the level of performance and help elevate that person's performance to that level. Too many times I've witnessed managers who taught a new (or worse – a seasoned) employee a task and then lamented that the employee couldn't perform it at a given level. The manager invariably taught just the basics and did nothing to raise the performance level to the desired capability. I believe this happens in part because the managers don't take into account the complexity to teach the task and therefore don't realize that they lack the ability to teach the task to the proper level.

You have to identify the level of performance and
help elevate that person's performance to that level.

Teaching is a task which is performed at different levels – there are bad teachers, good teachers, and the super-good teachers. The same will be said for any task to be performed. And the factors that dictate how well a person can and will perform a task are much broader than if they were taught well, but the complexity to teach is a definite consideration.

So far we have three of the four attributes. Frequency of performance, complexity to perform, and complexity to learn. If you couple the two complexities, you can fairly couple the last attribute with frequency.

Criticality – importance of getting it right the first time
In the Air Force, judging a task as high criticality was easy – just ask yourself if it involved loss of life or limb? All emergency procedures, by definition were high criticality. You couldn't afford to error when ejecting from a crashing aircraft. You had to get defusing ordinance correct the first time. Chances are you don't have too many life-threatening tasks on your MTL, but the concept is still valid. How important is it that you get that task right the very first time?

If you are presenting a sales pitch to a major client, how important is it that you get it right? The first time? Will you be able to bomb (see how I worked in the explosiveness?) with the client the first time and get a do-over? Or will your company lose a major client or sale?

In the Fall of 2010, Michigan State made a bold move against Notre Dame. Overtime. Notre Dame had scored only a field goal on their drive. Now Michigan State was stopped on third down and had to settle for a field goal to go to a double over-time. Well, they didn't *have* to. Instead Coach Mark Dantonio called for a pet play they had practiced all week, "Little Giants" (named after the movie). It was a fake field goal in which the holder took the snap and had to find a receiver. The first option wasn't available and he found the second choice. What made the play a highlight reel staple for the Spartans wasn't just the perfect execution, nor the surprise factor – Notre Dame never expected it. What made it special was that it was a high criticality task. If the play did not result in a touchdown, if the ball was knocked down, if the receiver dropped the pass, if it wasn't done right the first time…the game was over, and Michigan State loses. Done right the first time, they end up winning a shocker. It was (and still is) lauded as a "gutsy" call by Coach Dantonio. With it being a 46 yard field goal and his kicker being a first-year player, he actually felt more comfortable putting the pressure on his more experienced holder (and punter) and on the practice they had put in all week on the play. Regardless if it was gutsy, logical, or the only right call, it is a great example of a high criticality task.

Yes, risk is another way of looking at criticality.

Sometimes the risk or criticality is dependent upon the situation. Getting that play right the first time for Dantonio had a much higher criticality because if it failed the game was over. If he had tried the same play earlier in the game, when it wasn't a "do or die" situation, the criticality would be much lower. The specific situation was an important factor in the play's level of criticality. Another factor can be the audience or customer for the task.

A task of medium-to-low criticality can become high when the customer is a VIP. If you are fixing the phone for Joe in the office down the hall, it may not be critical that you get it right the first time…but if you're fixing the President of the company's phone, she may not be happy with having to have you redo it before she can use it.

If you have a range of criticality due to different audiences you have two choices:

1. Break the task out into a task for each type of audience OR
2. Use the highest level of criticality possible.

I suggest the second choice since the task is the same, a High Criticality will ensure you have all that you need in every possible situation or for any customer.

If you have trouble thinking of criticality, ask yourself is it acceptable for you to say you are finished and have to recant the claim and redo the work? If you can be called back and redo the task multiple times and no one will bite your head off for it, it's a low criticality. If you can only get it wrong two or three times before you get into trouble, medium. If you have to get it right the very first time, high. Remember to take into account your different audiences – if you normally do the task for very understanding, lenient people (perhaps you are the only one that knows you had to redo it – so you are your only critic), it would seem the task is low criticality. But if on occasion you perform it where others know and it would create a bad situation for you or the company, start climbing the scale toward high criticality.

Both frequency and criticality relate more to the type of training and the types of tools/instruments you should use, more than if training is required. The rating you give criticality will suggest if you would benefit from a checklist, quality checks or job aids. A task with high criticality may need all three – regardless if it requires training. In the Air Force we had Emergency Procedures which, regardless of how well or recently you had completed training had to be used when conducting the task.

*   H= if the task must be done right the first time
*   M= if you can take 2-3 times to get it right

- L = if you can take more than 3 tries to get it right

You discover even more when you combine the two factors.

When combined with Frequency, you can obtain guidance on *when* training (if required) should take place. If the task is Low Frequency and High Criticality, you should have the training "Just-In-Time" so that you will put the training to use while it is extremely fresh in your mind. You don't want to receive the training a month before you will use it.

Determining Results

So far I've avoided being "technical." Don't worry, while this will be more technical, it's still much better than any statistics book you'll read. Bear with me a little while, this won't be as painful as I just made it seem.

With the evaluation of these four attributes you can determine the following things for each task on your MTL:

1. Will training be necessary; is the item a training require- ment? This is the essence of the development plan. From the beginning you are looking to find which tasks the work- force carries out which will require training. If the worker is not able to perform at the level needed, will training resolve the gap in ability? In most cases if the task turns out to be a training requirement, that training will include an instructor in- stead of self-paced education. The Complexity to Perform and Complexity to Learn determine this result.

2. What type of training will be the best fit? There are different types of training to choose between – some require a purchase, some you can do in-house. Whatever you choose, it has to resolve gaps in ability.

   a. On-the-Job-Training (OJT) is just what it sounds like. Training that the worker receives on location, while performing the job. This may be the best type of training for any task because it allows for practical application and immediate feedback. Sometimes though this can be risky. Imagine if the task were flying an aircraft, especially a large airliner. Learning to pilot the craft "on-the-job" would be an extremely risky affair. OJT is another way of saying in-house, informal, one-on-one training. Hands-on training. If the Complexity to Learn is not high, OJT is a viable option.

   b. Just-in-Time Training (JITT) is another preferred method of delivery. You provide the training when needed. Rather than provide training on tax filing in June, you wait and provide that training at the end of March. This example points out the importance of doing a task breakdown. If the task is filling out tax forms – JITT and OJT dictates that you get the training when you fill out the forms. But, if the task is organize receipts for use in filing your taxes, you want that training January first (of the previous year)! If the frequency to perform is low and the criticality is high, JITT may be preferred.

   c. The need for Formal Classroom Training with textbooks, lectures, quizzes and tests is determined by the Complexity to Perform and Learn. If either is high, formal education with defined objectives and tests is recommended.

      d. Self-Paced Training is an option which is determined by the Complexity to Learn. If it's low, this may be a good option.

3. What tools/instruments would help? Tools or instruments *can* replace training, but in most cases you'll use them to supplement scheduled training. Workman's tools are used to enhance processes and make workers more effective and efficient. These tools are no different; except these are pre-scribed in response to the ratings you gave for the attributes. Most of these tools are dictated because of the infrequency and the criticality of the task. The less frequently a task is performed, the more a tool which provides instruction would help. The more critical the task, the more quality checks will help. I've listed four of the more common tools.

      a. Most times *Job Aids* are graphics which provide some guidance on how to perform a task. A common example you'll find is the "quick start" instructions which accompany a set of thorough instructions or user's manual. Most electronics come with these. The same type of tool for highlighting some key steps in a process is useful for tasks with a medium to high criticality, and is called for the lower the frequency.

      b. *Checklists* are called for when the criticality of a task is medium or high. If you can't afford to get it wrong, a checklist will help you to make sure you get it right.

      c. *Quality Checks* and quality assurance as a whole, are dictated when a task has a high criticality. The only way to ensure you get it right the first time is to, well, assure you get it right the first time. This means having someone do a quality check of the work. You can have as much formality as you need, from a "second pair of eyes" to a full blown Quality Assurance department.

d. *Thorough Instructions* (or manuals) are very useful and called for when the task has a low frequency and is a training requirement. Thorough instructions are never a "bad" thing and can benefit any process. But if the task is a training requirement and is performed infrequently, thorough instructions become a necessity.

NOTE: In the matching practicum chapter you'll find the table and accompanying formulas for determining the results.

A key aspect

There is one key aspect to the process I've outlined so far which may be worthy of a chapter of its own. You can follow all of the steps laid out to this point, and develop a very usable development plan. But, if you want to get the most out of your plan, and more specifically, get the most out of the journey of making the plan, you have to embrace collaboration.

To get the most out of the journey,
you must embrace collaboration.

Not only does the exercise of rating each task, based on four attributes, help the organization fully understand the position's requirements but it also forces managers and workers to communicate regularly and sincerely in an area critical to the success of both the organization and the individual.

You need to involve your workforce as much as possible – especially anyone who the development plan will affect. Many managers don't know how to build a positive rapport with their staff. If you collaborate fully with the person who will directly benefit from the development plan you will reap a ridiculously large amount of benefits.

You will learn what the worker feels about the job. You will learn what the worker feels about his performance, his knowledge level, and the difficulties in doing the job.

You also make one point crystal clear by collaborating…the development plan is a tool to help the worker improve performance and grow. It's not a management tool at all.

Don't wait to start this collaboration. Do it from the very beginning and continue throughout.

Do it together. Don't do it *for* the worker – it won't be perceived as a "favor," it'll be seen as a management-directed effort. Don't pass the process off to the workers to do alone – it won't be seen as empowerment, it'll be seen as a lack of interest in the workers' development.

Nope. This is strictly a team effort. This is *the* golden opportunity for the manager and worker to build a relationship around the most important facet of the workers' job. How well the worker performs the job is the most important thing because it will determine the quality of the relationship. The better the worker can perform the job, the more the manager will trust the worker. The more the manager trusts the worker, the happier everyone will be and consequently the better the relationship will be. The reason the worker is the organization's greatest asset is because the worker has the potential to excel at the job.

OK, hopefully that's more than enough preaching.

Chapter 2-3
Determine required skill levels

You now have a solid MTL to work from. You know the basic attributes for each task – the frequency with which they are performed, how important it is to perform it correctly the first time, how complex it is to perform and how complex it is to learn. With this knowledge, you also know which tasks require training and which don't. You know what tools may help with performing the task. If you've done all of this as a collaboration between the worker and the manager, you have gained a lot of benefit already. Now it's time to determine how well the training requirement tasks need to be performed.

You need to determine how well a task needs to be done by each position. You break the task requirements down into five skill levels; Novice (level 1) to Expert (level 5). The abilities and responsibilities build on each other.

1. Novice - At the novice level, the worker can barely perform the task. The worker needs supervision and guidance. Thorough instructions are necessary. While a worker may start as a novice, the required ability should never be at this level.
2. Beginner – At the beginner level, workers are expected to perform the task with limited supervision. The worker wouldn't have to know when they were getting the wrong results.
3. Skilled – The skilled level moves to an "unmanaged" state. The worker can perform the task without guidance or supervision. Most tasks fall into this level. The worker also knows when he is getting the wrong results, but doesn't know how to adjust to get the right results.
4. Supervisor – The supervisor level designates a worker who can train others. A worker at this level can supervise a beginner or novice, providing guidance as needed. This worker

understands how to resolve issues and troubleshoot problems.
5. Expert – The best. The expert level designates a worker who
    has mastered the task and can train others. She can evalu-
    ate the performance of levels 1 through 4.

For each task in the MTL, the manager should identify the level of
performance capability (skill) required. As a requirement, no tasks
should require the "novice" level and rarely will a position require a
worker to be an expert. You may find that you are lucky enough to
have an expert in your midst, but you won't normally *require* one.

I use a five-point scale to evaluate the capability required, but I encourage the use of whatever scale works for you. You can use a 10
or even 100 point scale. You need a method of communicating the
level of skill required.

As noted earlier, a key aspect of this entire process is to create this
plan in collaboration with the workers who will end up using the
plan. Find a way of differentiating between beginner and expert.
Feel free to have as wide a separation between these two levels as
you need. I'm partial to the five different markers of skill noted, but I
like to introduce the use of fractions in the five point scale. This allows me to have a simple delineation between a novice, beginner,
skilled, supervisor, and an expert while also allowing me to have
gradations of capability in between.

For example, fractions allow me to use the designation of 4.5 if it is
not clear if the rating should be a four or a five. If it's closer to the
definition of supervisor than expert, you could go with 4.25. It
doesn't matter.

What does matter is that you establish a performance level which
you can openly and clearly discuss with your employees. Now that

there is agreement of what tasks comprise the position, the manager and worker will come to an understanding of what levels of performance are expected. Again, this is a great opportunity for the manager and worker to understand the others' point of view.

Every job I've had so far would have been infinitely easier to perform if I knew up front what tasks were required and to what level of performance I was expected to achieve. These would seem to be obvious discussions to have between a manager and an employee, but they normally don't happen and if they do – never to the clear-cut level necessary.

This development plan will create these conversations early in the worker's employment.

Reality isn't settling

Here's an interesting question, "Why wouldn't you simply *require* the highest skill levels of all your workers?"

Usually because you can't afford it.

> The military has perfected this concept. There is a very strict process for being promoted. When the military needs to cut costs, the easiest way, fastest, and perhaps best way is to have a "Reduction-In-Force" (RIF). This is done by mostly pushing out higher skilled and higher paid military members while bringing in new recruits to fill the void. The new recruits are of course paid at the lowest salaries. They also start with little to no skills. So the military has one of the best professional development systems in the world and it's been effective for centuries.

Your organization probably can't afford to have everyone be an expert at every task. Most can't. And really, chances are you don't need it. You need a healthy mix of beginners and skilled workers. If you have one or two supervisor levels with an expert thrown in you probably have a highly effective team. Chances are you don't actually *need* an expert. If you have one, it's usually a luxury. And one you might not have for long as experts should be paid according to their capabilities, and some organizations are willing to pay what they are worth.

Most times, you need access to an expert, but you don't necessarily need one on the payroll. And you should never "need" a novice.

So, try to be realistic in your needs. How good do you really need the worker to be for each of the tasks? Don't pad the skills required. Be honest with your worker and with yourself.

Don't play down the skills required either. There are reasons why you might, and none of them are good. Regardless of your reasoning, they will be seen as manipulative.

Another sports analogy:

In football, if you have an outstanding defense, you may only need your quarterback to be a "game manager." No turnovers, safe and smart plays. No blunders. But if your defense is highly porous, you may need your quarterback to be a playmaker – a much higher skill level. If you look at a college team your quarterback needs may look like this:

1. Novice – nope. Like I said, you rarely "need" a novice. You'll take a talented one, but he won't get on the field until he has become better. Your "need" isn't for a novice although you'll recruit one and then plan to develop him.
2. Beginner – if your defense is superior and your running game is awesome, you may get away with a quarterback at this level. Probably this player is at best a backup while he's developing (also likely an underclassman).
3. Skilled – this is what most colleges require of their starting quarterback. This is the minimum to get on the field. Still the

backup, but as a coach you'll get him some experience when you can since if the starter is unable to play, you have to go with this player.

4. Supervisor – the starting quarterback *needs* to be able to train others. The quarterback at this level gets all of the offensive players in the right position, can audible at the line based on the defensive set, and manages the clock. Every team would like to have a player at this level. Actually to be an elite team, you want all your starters to be at this level of performance. You'd also like your players to be bigger and faster than your opponents, but while you can't make them any taller (and only slightly faster), you can develop their skills.

5. Expert – this is *not* required. I can't think of a coach that would require this of his starter. Imagine if it was required and the starter was injured? What are the chances that the backup would be skilled? Or be an expert? No, it is the rare situation when you find yourself with an expert level quarterback at the college level. These are the Heisman Trophy candidates. These are the first-round, top 3 picks in the draft. These are the players who get to play the Sunday after they graduate – not just on Sundays, but right away. And just like in the business world, if you have an expert at any position, chances are they'll leave your organization early for greener pastures.

I hope this analogy helps. As you may have noticed, the sports analogy is more than a running metaphor.

The concepts in this book fully apply to any organization and to any team. Sports or business. Academic or military.

When you look at an undersized team (any of the military acade-mies will do) you may wonder how they ever compete with the "big boys." All three academies are Division I BCS schools! And all three have weight limits which make it impossible to have the same size as almost every team they play. Even so, they compete. They de-velop the players they have to help them play at the highest level they can. Then they run systems that maximize their strengths and minimize their weaknesses.

They compete.

They compete well.

Any organization can do the same.

The process

While I've given you a lot of guidance on where to find the evalua-tors, and even how to do the evaluation, it's time to cover how to get the "answer." What rating do you put for each task? It's definitely *not* the average of all responses.

It's much more personal than that. I want you to sit down with your worker, the two of you together. I want you to use any other assess-ments that you deem helpful as inputs. I want you to use the man-ager's and worker's assessments as the base. This foundation and the other input should be used as the basis for the final ratings for each task. This should be a healthy and useful conversation. Since you are determining the requirement for each task for a given posi-tion – this is a great time to have a collaborative session with all of your workers filling the position. Don't worry if the worker is a novice or an expert you can learn from each other.

There are distinct considerations when evaluating the tasks which allow you to personalize the development plan at every stage. The first was the Master Task List. Even though the positions may seem the same and you may have used the same job description to hire your staff, the MTL helps you to see where the workers are inter-changeable and where they are not. The second opportunity for clarifying the differences between seemingly similar positions was the four attributes. One worker may perform a task daily while an-other may only do that task every other month. The criticality for a task performed by one worker who directly supports the president of the company may be much higher than the exact same task per-formed for internal customers.

The evaluation of the required skill level for a position is another op-portunity for this specificity. Even if the workers are the same grade, there is the possibility that their required level of skill at performing a given task may differ. It is expected for this difference to exist when the tasks are performed by workers of varying grades, but I've found it also differs amongst those of the same level of responsibility. This happens naturally when you have a larger team and the tasks are distributed between the staff. It also happens when you find a posi-tion existing in different units. How one unit leverages the position may differ drastically from how another does. All of this helps in de-fining each role. Each role is special and each worker provides spe-cific benefits to the organization.

Back to the list.

As a rule, you should have a healthy amount of tasks to assess. I'm expecting that you found a few tasks needing a task breakdown. I also expect that you *found* some tasks you didn't know were in-cluded in the position. Since you have a lot of tasks, and hopefully a decent amount of input, I want you to spend no more than 3 minutes on a task.

Look at the scores given by the workers and the supervisor (normally you). Take a quick first step:

1. Are the scores the same? If so, capture it and move on to the next task.
2. If they are not the same, have a short discussion of why each scored it the way she did. Usually the discussion goes something like; "I thought it requires a 3 because" and "but John does it and he's obviously only a 2." This is another opportunity to improve communications.
    a. Spend no more than 3 minutes.
    b. If you come to an agreement, put that score down.
    c. If you can't agree, take the higher score regardless of who is championing it and move on. You'll always be able to revisit in the future.
    d. Don't simply average the scores. This is not the time for compromise. You are seeking collaboration instead.

Remember, the biggest benefit you will get is from the discussion, so don't overthink the scoring. You'll take the higher score here, choosing to "err on the side of excellence." Capture these ratings so you can use them later.

Chapter 2-4
Evaluate existing abilities

You now have a solid MTL, attributes for each task, information on which tasks are training requirements, what tools/instruments would help, and what type of training best fits each task. You've then developed a rating for the required skill-level for each task. You now have a positional development plan. This is a valuable asset for an organization. It can be used to create a meaningful job posting. It can be used to identify training programs. It can also be used for building career plans and cross training strategies. At a minimum, it can be used to bolster the self-esteem of your staff and provide clarity to management of what makes up the business. This is worth relishing.

Use this achievement as a springboard to even bigger things. Use it to improve processes and get better hires. Use it to justify resources and ensure equitable pay scales. But, remember that it's not the final deliverable. This is a benefit or byproduct of your journey to developing personal professional development plans. Granted, if you are building the plan for a position which you have not filled yet, you actually have gone as far as you can. But, once you have someone to develop professionally, you'll need to get to the next step.

All of this was accomplished as a team, fully involving the workers and the manager. Everything up to this point should have been *safe* and easily accepted by all. There were no chances for hurt feelings.

Yup, now is the first time that you are likely to encounter a little resistance.

The idea was to provide a good basis and foundation for the manager-worker relationship. If you've done this well, this next step should be seen as a logical progression and shouldn't cause any stress. But I'm not naïve enough to think there won't be some stress anyway. So take your time here. Be ready to review the process and go over the guidelines again.

Ok, let's get started.

You're going to do an evaluation of each worker's current skill level in relation to each task. By looking at the capability level of the worker, you see even more clearly how the task-centered focus "gets 'er done." Now that you know what is required of each position, at the task level, you can evaluate how skilled your current workforce is.

The performance of a task will reflect the understanding and knowledge of the worker. The following criteria for evaluation increases in importance as you move from one to five. Here's another, perhaps simpler way to look at the five levels.

1. Novice - Can you perform the task?
2. Beginner - Can you perform it well? (minimal errors)
3. Skilled - Can you perform it efficiently? (with minimal effort)
4. Supervisor - Can you perform it quickly and can you show others how to perform it?
5. Expert - Can you adjust to changes on the fly?

I'm happy with calling the beginner level – "developing." It reflects that the worker can do the job but requires help from time to time. Remember – the name you call it doesn't matter. It doesn't matter if you have 4 or 6 levels. What matters is that you analyze your requirements ahead of time and discuss them with the people filling the positions.

Now that you've defined the requirements for the position, it's time to do a similar assessment of the employees' current abilities. This is the beginning of the personal development plan or individual professional development plan. Each employee gets their own version of the MTL and therefore the plan.

This is a good opportunity to leverage some of the concepts that have been developed for providing feedback in the workplace. The really fun part is that where the feedback tools usually have to be carefully implemented – they run the risk of offending those receiving the feedback – in this case it's much less contentious. The rating you receive as feedback is less a reflection of your personality, personage, or even behavior. It's truly a measure of your ability.

One simple example is the worker who is underperforming. You have a highly skilled worker who for reasons you won't venture to guess, is not performing up to his ability. When you rate their capabilities – ability to perform each task, you may rate them much higher than they are performing. No reason to get defensive there! If the person is performing at a 2 level, but you believe he has the ability to perform at a 4 level, you rate their capability at 4. It's for a later discussion between the manager and the employee why they perform below their capability. By the way, that is one of the benefits of the development plan I'll present later.

So, the method for gathering inputs for this step I was referring to is known as a 360 degree review. The simple translation is to gather inputs on each employee's capabilities using the same 5-point scale, with the same definitions for each level, you used in defining the positional requirements.

Have the manager and the worker assess the worker's ability to perform the task – again separately. Now add in a good sampling of assessments from peers of the worker. If these peers also do the same job, they'll have the opportunity to rate each other. Besides the intended use, you'll find an excellent by-product in that you will have new insight to how each worker sees the other in terms of skill level. Of course there are other factors which make a worker a good employee and a respected colleague. But now you'll have insight to how each sees the other in terms of expertise.

The better you know your workforce the better you can interact and lead them.

I'm not suggesting this replace the real need for the manager to "spend time" with his workers and getting to know them. On the contrary, this is just one more source of information the manager can leverage and a means of getting to know him better.

Remember, the journey is the biggest benefit from creating a development plan.

This is a great tool for a sports team. Regardless of the level; high school, college, minor league, or pro, the coach and player will both benefit greatly from this assessment. One of the first things I do when I coach a volleyball team is ask each player to self-assess their overall skill level. I also ask them to specifically identify their strengths and weaknesses. After I get this feedback I provide them with an MTL for the position they'll be filling and ask them to assess their skill levels for each task. The difference is staggering. I'll have players who say they are highly skilled, top-of-the-line performers when I ask the general question.

When I present them with a detailed list of tasks and ask them to assess their abilities to perform each, they invariably end up being a much lower level than they thought. Sometimes it works the other way. I'll have some modest players who say they are "alright" and then when they assess the skills needed for the position it turns out that they are much better than they thought. This provides great insight to their confidence and education. When I share my evaluation with them, they learn a lot about what I see in them. They find out the potential I see and what I think they need to work on. This is a great way to start the coach-player relationship.

So, you should now have the manager's, worker's, and the worker's peers' assessments of the worker's capabilities for each task. Or in the case of a team; the coach's, assistant coaches', player's, and the player's teammates assessments.

There are a couple more people who can be asked to participate. If the employee has subordinates, workers who report to her, they can be asked to fill out an assessment also. You may get a few "I don't knows" in the responses but that's alright. Again, this provides great input to the worker and the manager of the worker's abilities – and how others see the worker. Unlike personality indicators and other "soft" stuff it is much easier to be objective with these measures.

A final participant in the exercise can be customers. Depending on the relationship between the employee and her customers, this may be a great source of insight for the manager and the employee alike. When you decide to include external customers you'll of course have to take into consideration the relationship between your company and the customer, and the relationship between the particular employee and the customer.

Regardless of the position, there are normally also internal customers. This can be another great source of feedback about the capabilities of the worker and the organization.

Each of these sources of feedback can provide valuable insights for the employee and the manager. Once you've collected this feedback, it's time to put a score on the form so you can identify gaps between the requirement and the capability of the worker. Wherever you find negative gaps (deficiencies) you will have an opportunity for development.

While you can gather feedback from as many sources as you like, you must have ratings from the worker and the supervisor at a minimum.

The process

I suggest you use a similar process to that for coming to agreement on the positional requirements, to come to agreement on the individual's ratings. Use a maximum of 3 minutes for each task, where the supervisor and worker don't agree, and once again pull in other viewpoints as input to the discussion.

At the end of the three minutes, if you can't come to a consensus, you want to take the lowest rating. In the case of the requirement – you erred on the side of excellence by taking the higher score. That means even if you chose wrong, and made the task a higher skill requirement than necessary, the only harm will be that you think you need a higher skill level than you really do. This will wash out over time. If you go the other way, you may stop developing your staff prematurely.

In the case of the individual's capabilities, you err on the side of excellence by choosing the lower score regardless of who is championing it because our worst consequence will be that you try to develop the worker when his skills are already adequate.

I've found over the years that workers tend to downplay their abilities rather than "pad their scores." The reasons vary from humility to misunderstanding the task. Sometimes it's false humility – a sign that the worker lacks self-esteem or the manager hasn't created a culture of recognition. It really doesn't matter why. What does matter is that this is a great opportunity to build a relationship. Here and now I give you full permission to ignore the 3 minute rule if you are having a fruitful discussion. Don't let the guidelines I suggest keep you from reaping the benefits of creating a development plan.

It's worth a note here that a facilitator (some would say mediator) will help this process immensely. It doesn't have to be a specialist or training expert...but it helps to have a third party present to:

1. Keep the discussion from falling down any Alice-in-Wonderland rabbit holes.
2. Remind the participants to err on the side of excellence – take the lower of the scores when they can't agree in a timely fashion.
3. Keep the discussion to the 3-minute limit. A stopwatch isn't required but it helps to have an eye on the clock.
4. Keep the conversation focused on the assessment of capability not past performance.

Recap

At this point you should have the following artifacts:

1. A list of tasks which make up the responsibilities for a given position, the MTL.
2. An assessment of the four key attributes for each task for a given position:
   a. How frequently the task is performed
   b. How important it is to perform the task correctly the first time

   c. How complex the task is to perform

   d. How complex the task is to teach

3. A determination for each task – if it is a training requirement or not

4. Suggestions for how to train to each task

5. Suggestions for tools/instruments for performing each task

6. An assessment of how well each task needs to be performed for the position (positional development plan)

7. An assessment of how well each worker *can* currently perform each task

You now have the basis for a personal professional development plan. These artifacts should be documented. They can be shared with others.

But, of course, there is more to be done. You haven't actually found any training, scheduled any training, nor improved your employees' abilities to perform any tasks.

Before you finish the development plan, before you "close the loop," let's stop and review what you have achieved. The artifacts listed previously could be considered byproducts of the process. The real value to what you've done so far are important benefits which I want to ensure you don't miss out on.

The key is communication

As mentioned earlier, when you identified the tasks for a given position, if you involved those who currently fill that position you open the door to meaningful conversation around what defines the position. This type of conversation is useful to both the manager and the worker. Besides sharing the knowledge of what each believes the position entails, by having the conversation, you create an atmosphere of willing participation around understanding the job. And this leads to a greater understanding of the department or unit and ultimately a real investment in the organization. I hear all the time that you want your workers to be an "engaged workforce." You want them to "take ownership" of their job and the organization. This isn't possible if the worker doesn't have enough of the big picture. And it's impossible if the worker or manager doesn't understand the tasks which make up the job, or the positions which make up the department, or how the departments fit into the organization.

This healthy conversation will continue as the manager and employee work through the process. Together they will determine the frequency, criticality and complexities of the tasks. I've seen this be a powerful tool for teaming. Just the discussion around each attribute garnishes great benefits to the organization. After over 30 years of experience in the workforce, it doesn't surprise me that managers don't know the frequency the worker performs a task. Actually many managers don't know all of the tasks which comprise the job and frequently think the worker performs tasks which either were actually done by others or not done at all. You can take this as a sign of poor management – a lack of interest in what the worker does day in and day out. Or you can be a "glass-half-full" person and figure it's actually a reflection of how autonomous your skilled workforce has become. Or that managers have grown to trust their workers. Or that the only real important thing is that the job gets done and as long as things are running smoothly, there isn't any reason to know more about the position.

Of course these would be pretty lame excuses for not getting to know the worker and not knowing the position's requirements. A good manager, like a good coach, makes the worker better. A good manager clears the path of obstacles so the worker can excel. A good manager doesn't need to be able to perform every job or know how to do tasks – but the manager has to know what those tasks are and how well the worker can perform them.

A good manager, like a good coach,
makes the worker better.

The prevailing disconnect I've seen between the manager's under-standing of the workers' jobs is worsened by the lack of communica-tion between the two. It's been said that the worker's happiness with a job is a direct result of the quality of the manager. I agree but be-lieve it goes a little further. The quality of the manager is best deter-mined by the ability of the worker to "talk to" the manager about the day-to-day issues of the job. If the worker feels safe and comforta-ble having conversations with his boss, the relationship will grow and the worker will be happy. Creating a development plan using the process documented here provides that vehicle for more healthy conversations.

Once the worker *knows* the manager understands what goes into filling the position the worker starts to have confidence that the man-ager cares. Someone can't care about something they don't know exists or doesn't understand.

Once the manager *knows* the worker understands the level of per-formance expected of the position the manager starts to believe that the worker cares about doing the job and doing it well.

Once the manager and worker come to agreement on where the worker needs additional training to improve performance capabili-ties, both begin to believe that they are sharing common goals – performing the job to clearly stated levels.

The benefits are simple but "priceless"

    a. Building an MTL for the position helps everyone gain a better understanding of what the position entails.

    b. Evaluating performance requirements creates healthy conversation about what the job really is, and the manager's expectations.

    c. Evaluating worker capabilities

        i. creates healthy conversation around what will help the worker perform better and what management can do to help and

        ii. creates healthy conversation around the managers perception of the worker's capabilities compared to the worker's perception of her own abilities

Chapter 2-5
Gap management

Identify the gaps in ability

The focus moves now from creating the plan to executing it; to *getting the job done.* Now that you know where the deficiencies are, you can address them with training and improve the worker's ability to perform the job.

As the head coach, you've identified what you need from each player in each position. You've identified the deficiencies. It's time to prepare the team for the upcoming season opener. Of course, the development doesn't stop at that point. You have to continue developing each player throughout their time under your care.

Oh that managers would look at their workers this way.

It's worth a mention here that I've had to deal with "political correctness" throughout my work in organizational development. I've been told that the use of the word "deficiencies" will possibly make a worker feel bad. I've been told to find a more friendly term to depict when the requirements for the job are higher than the capabilities of the person. Perhaps, "opportunity for training" would work.

I believe the overuse of political correctness is stymying the ability of most people to communicate clearly. Throughout both of my first two books, I argue that clarity of language is the foundational building block to changing the way things get done. This lack of clarity can only be compounded with the push to carefully avoid ever insulting or offending anyone...even if you are speaking the truth.

It may be my favorite biblical quote of all time...Jesus said, "If I speak the truth, why do you strike me?" He wasn't worried about political correctness. He spoke the truth. He did so with love and kindness in his heart, but he pulled no punches. I figure He's a good role model.

Since you follow the principle of erring on the side of excellence, and you took the higher of the scores for the required performance level and took the lower of the scores for the current ability levels (where you couldn't agree quickly), you are assured not to miss any potential gaps in capability.

Following this simple principle allows the workers to identify the gaps in their capability without becoming overly sensitive about any deficiencies. The *worst* case scenario for the worker is that he will get training he doesn't really need. While the top priority is to identify the deficiencies, another valuable by-product is the identification of workers whose capabilities to perform certain tasks are above and beyond the requirement. These strengths can be used to identify in-house trainers. When managers decide to take advantage of in-house training (some of the analysis will recommend it) there are multiple benefits to the organization.

- The organization will save funding by providing training in-house.
- The worker-as-trainer rightfully gains recognition for her strengths.
- The manager learns the strengths of each worker and can leverage these strengths when making assignments or forming teams.
- Depending on the situation, the manager may elect to change the requirements for the individuals – so that workers can focus on their strengths. It may not be necessary for everyone in the same position to have the same ability levels.

- Teaching is one of the best ways to improve a skill set, so by providing training in-house, both participants (trainer and trainee) improve their skills.

Now that you know where the gaps are, you need to decide which gaps to address first.

Prioritizing the gaps
Which gaps should you address first?

This isn't as easy at is sounds. You end up asking a lot of questions, trying to determine what order to train. Should you set your priorities solely on criticality? On complexity? Does frequency matter?

When you set priorities you can take all of the four attributes into account, but you'll also want to look at when the task will next be performed. And what level of capability you will need at that time.

Other things to consider will be the availability of training. If you have determined that formal training is necessary, you will be handcuffed by that training's availability. This is one of the strengths of self-paced training. So, the *need* rightfully dictates the priority, tempered by the ability to get the training. Even a high need item can become a lower priority if the training just won't be available until a later date.

But is "priority" equal to "importance?" The purist will say the priority doesn't change due to the availability. The priority remains the same although you may have to schedule lower priority tasks before the top priority items. So, it may be more accurate to say we are going to "order" the tasks using the priority, the availability, and when the training is needed to schedule it.

Setting the order will help everyone involved know when the training should occur and the relative importance of reaching the desired level of performance for the task. It is also another opportunity for conversation.

With so many considerations it helps to have a few critical things to guide your thinking.

The order will be determined by evaluating the following factors:

1. The importance of getting the training sooner rather than later
2. The availability of the training including
    a. The costs
    b. The availability of the instructors/materials
    c. The availability of the worker
3. The timing of the task
4. The level of capability of the other workers
5. The availability of the other workers
6. The complexity of the task – how long it will take to learn

When you look at all of these factors you may say, "that didn't help at all!" And you may be right. The bottom line for setting the priorities is the manager (with the worker's input) has to identify which tasks need to be trained first, second, third, and so on. The six criteria I offered was intended to help, but they aren't a formula. Hey, I gave you formulas for the task analysis – now you have to make some decisions on your own.

> Each organization is different and each situation is unique is an obvious statement. But unfortunately, it's so obvious that we occasionally forget it. You will need to develop your own plans. You will have to find out what works for you and your organization. The easy way (using plans from other organizations) isn't always the best way.

If you have a strong defense and let's throw in a strong running game, you may have other needs ahead of developing your quarterback's ability to throw the long ball. You will want to develop the quarterback in all facets, but the top priority may not be this skill. Actually, the top priority may not be your quarterback. While your goal is to develop everyone to their potential and thereby make your organization as strong as possible, you will have to decide on the right sequence. This is due to the lack of resources (time, money, manpower, etc.) that we all struggle with.

So you need to look at each situation and make the right call. You will be able to train some personnel simultaneously. You may be able to develop multiple skills for a specific person simultaneously. There isn't a set of rules for dealing with the multitude of factors you may encounter.

While I don't have formulas for selecting the ordering of each training need, I *can* give you more on each of the criteria. A simple way to look at it is figuring out which skill you should develop in your worker. As with any position, the key to answering this question may be determining what the team needs and when they need it.

The importance of getting the training sooner rather than later
You need to decide how important it is that the worker gain the necessary skills now rather than later. What is driving the immediacy of the training? Is it a task which has to be performed sooner rather than later? Is it for a project or contract which has to be fulfilled in the near future? If you can't get your staff up-to-speed on the task you may have to hire temporary workers or subcontract the work.

Hopefully there are very few tasks which you need your workers to perform right away which they are incapable of. Chances are you will have already addressed these.

Availability

The availability of the training including costs, instructors/materials, and the worker. Obviously if you don't have the resources required to do the training, you can't get it done at this time. If the source you want to use costs too much for your current budget – you either have to work around this or wait. You can try to find less expensive sources for the training. You can change the method from one you're paying for to doing it in-house. Of course you still end up *paying* for the training, but it won't come out of your training budget. The availability of the instructor and materials can be dealt with the same way.

But the availability of the worker can't be mitigated. If the trainee is not available, you really can't do anything but wait or find ways to free up her time. If she has a full schedule and no time to do the training, you can take some things off her plate and hopefully free up enough time. If she is on vacation or already engaged in training you may have to simply wait.

Availability of the worker is a critical path in determining the timing (and prioritization) of the training. Everything else can be negotiated.

In scheduling training – the availability of the worker is critical. Everything else can be negotiated.

Timing of the Task

Ask yourself a few questions to help determine the order. Is this a periodic task? Does it only occur infrequently? Is it coming up soon? If it's an annual task, and won't be due for another 9 months, it can become a lower priority. If it's a weekly or daily task, you may want to bump it up toward the front of the line.

Capability of the other workers

This speaks to how important it is for worker X to obtain the necessary skills. If you already have one or more workers who can perform the task to requirement, your *need* for worker X to obtain the skill may be much less critical. Just because the task is associated with a specific position, everyone filling the position doesn't have to have that skill. This may seem odd. If the MTL for the position includes the task, why wouldn't you need a worker to have that capability?

For some of us this may be a totally new concept – just because a position includes a specific task that doesn't mean that everyone who fills that position needs to do that task. That's why you have specialties.

Think of running backs. Even though you may want them all to know the entire playbook and be able to execute all of the tasks...you can work around it if they don't. Notre Dame produced a good example of this in the 2013 season. One of our receivers excelled at blocking...a skill the coaching staff would have loved for all of the receivers to have. This receiver was below the level of proficiency they would have liked at running certain routes. But his ability to block got him into games.

Unfortunately it became a known quantity that when this player was in the game he was there to block, which meant the plays you could expect were predictable. The surprise play would be to throw to this player rather than run a screen or a running play in which his ability to block would be required. This is an extreme example – and one that eventually kept him off the field because teams knew what to expect. But this example plays out in other circumstances and teams. There is the blocking back. There is the running quarterback or as in the case of Notre Dame's quarterback for 2013 – the non-running variety. Blake Bell for Oklahoma in 2012 came into games when they needed short-yardage gains...he was so much a running quarterback and so *not* a passing one that his tasks were limited to a small package of plays. Granted, the next year, after improving his skill set he became what they call a dual threat quarterback.

Some players never attain all of the skills required for a given position. Most though develop a passable level of skill for all the required tasks. Just as you may have players who can't perform all of the required tasks of a position, you also may find that even if they can perform all the tasks, they can't necessarily perform them to the skill level desired.

When a coach encounters a player who can't perform to a desired level he doesn't abandon that player unless he has a ready replacement on the team. A good coach takes his best player and finds a way to help him excel, even if it means modifying the job. You can do the same.

But don't settle. That's what this book is about, creating a plan for developing your workforce so you can have the best possible team with everyone reaching their potential.

There is always room for customizing a job or position to fit the talent you have.

Availability of the other workers

I already covered the possibility that other workers may be able to perform the tasks, but this covers the concern that other workers may be needed to fill-in for the trainee while she is improving her skillset.

Some training may require time away from the job, away from the organization. In this case, you'll need to have any critical responsibilities covered.

How long will it take?

The complexity of the task – how long it will take to learn may also be a consideration for you. If it's something that can be learned in a week, scheduling may be easier than fulfilling a need which takes a month's worth of training. You can put other complex skillsets into this category also. Perhaps a task requires the worker to obtain theories and concepts which increase the time and complexity to learn. Like having to learn how to code in Java Script. Or running a highly complex piece of machinery. These are extreme cases which you will have probably already accounted for – like having an indoctrination program in place for new hires. I thought it was worth inclusion none-the-less.

Remember that jobs constantly change as do the tasks that make them up. A new task may require new skills which in turn fit outside of your established norms and procedures.

Critical point

By developing the MTL together, as a team, everyone reaps benefits from the process from the very beginning. This is why you have to include all players – regardless of who knows the answers better; both management and employees will benefit from the process. Imagine the conversations:

- "I didn't know you did that"
- "I didn't realize that was that complex"
- "I didn't realize you thought that was so easy to do"
- "You do that daily?"
- "You automated that? I thought you still took hours to do that"

By developing the MTL together, the supervisor gets a full picture of what goes into fulfilling the position. The employee gets the affirmation that the boss actually knows (depending on the level of involvement you could say "understands") what the worker does for a living. This is worth the effort of developing a plan all by itself. But wait, there are more benefits to be realized!

Chapter 2-6
Selecting training vehicles

You have all the information you need. You have a comprehensive Master Task List, you have attributes rated for each task so that you have recommendations about tools, job aids, and the type of training which should be used. You have evaluated the skill level required for the position and how well your worker fills that role's requirements. Filling and thereby removing that gap is the measure of success of any professional development plan. Now is when all of your preparation is put to work.

President Lincoln said, if he were given six hours to chop down a tree, he'd spend four hours sharpening his axe. It is important for us to understand that to have a living professional development plan, you have to have a solid, robust, and comprehensive foundation.

It's time to find the training vehicles to span those gaps. This can be as enjoyable as building an MTL can be tedious. You're looking for training offerings; seminars, classes, webinars, podcasts and Computer-Based-Training. You can even learn a lot via YouTube now-a-days. You can take advantage of On-the-Job training, recognizing your experts as you leverage their knowledge. There are books, study guides, and manuals.

A relatively new and big player in the training arena is online training. This includes everything from webinars, to podcasts, to instructor-led online courses. Online training has opened many opportunities for fulfilling training needs.

I'm not going to recommend any specific training organizations. Not only are there too many possible topics/areas to cover, but the quality of each can change over time. Instead I suggest that when you close the loop in the next step (evaluating the training) you make your own list of sources which you like and work for you. And maybe more importantly those that don't. Then share that with your peers.

So rather than give you a list of recommendations which will be out of date by the time this gets published, let's look at the types of vehicles you have to choose from, and some of the pros and cons you can use, to select the best fit for you and your organization.

Selecting the type of training

Go back to our four attributes and the resulting recommendations. What is the type of training recommended?

Formal classroom training

This may be the most common form of training that comes to mind. You can find this training through your local college or university. You can also find some through specialty training organizations or technical schools. Some highly technical training is available from certified sources which do almost nothing but provide training.

If you choose this method, don't lock yourself into attending only scheduled classes – you may find that the offerings don't work for you due to time, location, or cost. Keep open to bringing an instructor to your location to teach the course on site. This is a great benefit of knowing all of your workers' tasks, required capability levels, and gaps. Many times a task, or the supporting skills/knowledge needed for a task, is performed by multiple positions in the organization – many times not on the same team or even in the same department. By having professional development plans across the organization management can leverage the common tasks or requirements to group training efforts.

This cross-knowledge, made possible by the MTLs can also be leveraged in other ways. If a worker is out for an extended period of time, finding a backfill within the organization is much easier when you know the tasks performed by the entire workforce.

The more development plans are instituted across the organization the more value each plan has. Not only will there be outstanding communications throughout the organization, there will be a wealth of documented information about each job. You will learn how positions are alike and how they differ.

Development plans help the organization exponentially.
The more you have the more you get.

One consideration is the effectiveness of the training received. How well the training satisfies the needs of the organization can be a strong factor in choosing the proper training method.

On-the-Job-Training

On-the-job-training is usually conducted by in-house expertise, but it can be taught by an outside instructor brought onto site. The major benefit to this training is that it is very task-centric. Performance of the task is explained, demonstrated, practiced, and then tested. This is especially prevalent in hands-on tasks like manufacturing or physical labor. This type of training is great when combined with the theoretical. Besides working on the task being learned, there is a comfort level of being at the job. The worker quickly sees how the improvement in performance relates to the job.

Think of all of the seminars you've attended where you thought, "I can't wait to get back to work to try that out!" With on-the-job-training, you are always on the job, trying it out.

Remember, all forms of training need to be evaluated for effectiveness. Many managers think this is the best way to train because:

1. It's less expensive, especially if you use in-house instructors

2. It is easier to schedule
3. The manager and worker can see improvement as soon as it happens
4. It is much easier to teach

Which do you think is untrue?

If you said four, "it is much easier to teach" you'd be right. This is a misconception many people have. Many managers believe anyone who performs the task at a given skill level should be able to teach a coworker to perform at the same level. If you review the skill levels you used you'll see that only the highest level of skill was strong enough to teach the skill – at any level. Even then, there are talents and skills required to be a good teacher which a subject matter expert may not possess. Teaching is a specialized skill in itself, regardless of the material being taught.

When the manager becomes frustrated with the worker's inability to learn from a peer, the next common error is for the manager to fix the problem by conducting the training himself. Unfortunately, being a manager doesn't automatically make someone a good teacher. Usually when this fails also, the manager decides it *must* be the worker's fault and things quickly move downhill from there.

Remember, although it may be less expensive, able to be scheduled as you see fit, and you can see progress quickly – it doesn't make it *easier* to do.

All of this is more obvious in sports. You can send your players off to specialists for specific skills. Players at all levels benefit from individual tutelage. Almost all teams utilize "in-house" training. Most serious teams bring in special instructors on occasion for some special in-house sessions.

At the college level and above, formal training (still in-house though) is prevalent. The biggest obstruction to Coach Brian Kelly implementing his offense at Notre Dame may have been the inability for the quarterback's to pick up the intricacies of the playbook. For the first 3 to 4 years the local sports talk shows would say, "once the quarterback gets it, Coach Kelly will be able to open up the entire playbook." Up until then, Coach Kelly made it clear that there was a significant amount of plays that were not being used. Part of that is due to the abilities of the players. Another factor though is the ability of the players to comprehend the system and the plays.

Even in sports, classroom work can be necessary.

Self-paced training/Computer-based-training

Self-paced training is perfect for some tasks. It is usually one of the least expensive methods of training but it is also difficult for the worker – especially if the worker lacks self-discipline. This type of training includes everything from following a manual or thorough instructions to taking on-line or computer-based training. If you choose this route, you'll still need to have an expert available to answer questions and to evaluate the effectiveness of the training.

Besides a specific expert, many times you can find assistance from user-groups, Listservs, or discussion groups online. This training, when done well, can be very rewarding and long-lasting. The worker, having done it all on his own, feels a high level of accomplishment. Also, since the worker had to figure out a good amount on his own the lessons learned will stick better.

There are of course other methods; role-based, game theory, and scenario-based training come to mind – but the ones I've covered are the ones I've found to be the most common.

Usually this is best for keeping a set of skills up-to-date. It works better if the trainee has a good foundation of skills. I like this for refresher training and for introducing new concepts or tasks to a highly skilled worker. When I wanted to expand my knowledge base on metrics, I would normally end up buying a book or two. But when I first started, I couldn't have done it from a book alone. I learned more than I could have hoped, and faster than I would have expected by having a mentor work with me on-the-job.

I coach in an organization which believes in helping coaches develop throughout their careers. I've helped other coaches and I've been helped by peers and more experienced coaches. You also pay to have your coaches attend seminars offered by some of the best coaches in the industry.

With mentorship and years of years of experience as a strong foundation, I now find a lot of benefit in watching the occasional video on how to coach a specific skill. Or a video on how to perform a task. I get much more from these self-guided tools than I would have when I first started coaching.

Combinations

It should go without saying that any of the types of training listed can be combined. The more complex the task to perform and/or teach, the more likely you'll benefit from a combination of the types of training. Sometimes it depends on the level of the worker and the level of required skill. As I mentioned, once you have a certain level of experience, you can teach a task in a more self-guided method. Also you'll find that people learn differently. Some need direct human interaction for it to stick. Others don't. Some need hands-on practice, while others only need to see it done - even if it's a video.

The point is, don't get locked into one type of training or one vendor for your needs. This is definitely a good time to keep an open mind. Even if you evaluate the training source as being superior, it still has to match the learning style of your worker.

Again, by involving the workers throughout, you'll side step some of the possible issues you can run into.

Just-In-Time training

This one isn't really a different form of training, but a possible attribute of any of the methods listed earlier. Just-in-time training is well titled as it describes accurately what it is. When the task needs to be performed, the worker is trained on it. Either right before or during the task's scheduled performance. This concept ensures that the training is timely and has the benefit of total relevance for the worker. Chances are you've taken advantage of this already on small, simple tasks. You may sit down with the worker and explain how to do a task – because they need to get it done and they don't know how.

You may have used the concept when showing someone how to do a task for you because they are backfilling for you while you go on vacation. Chances are you wait until the task needs to be done right before you leave and you step the person through the process. If it was a more complex task you probably had them perform it a few times before you left. I recently had someone stand in for me while I left for a week-long vacation. I showed her how to do the daily task a week before I left. I wanted her to practice for that last week with me present to help her through any hiccups before I left.

If the employee is having trouble *getting it,* try a different method as well as trying different vendors.

Selecting the vendor

Now that you have decided on the type of training, you'll want to choose your vendor wisely. When you are paying for the training, it is your responsibility to pick a quality vendor. The best advice is to find a vendor which delivers measurable value for your training dollars. This means that the vendor is less on the hook than you are. You have to evaluate the effectiveness of the training so that you can make intelligent decisions.

The biggest mistake I've seen in professional development programs is the lack of an evaluation of the training received. I'll cover this specifically, but it's important enough to include here – the selection of your training vehicle is the best way to ensure you get a good return for your investment.

My wife, who was very slow to embrace the recent advances in technology, has become an expert at comparison shopping online. She actually schools *me* on how to use product reviews by customers before I buy. Why not do the same with your training choices?

Ask for references. Really. Most times I get the impression that vendors and specific training are selected simply by the quality of the marketing materials. If a vendor sends you an advertisement for a course which may fill a recently identified need, the only question most ask is; "would you like to attend this training?" The more involved supervisor will first ask if the training is needed, and then ask if the worker wants the training. This very informal selection process exists because most managers lack a solid understanding of what goes into a given position. You don't have that excuse any longer.

You no longer respond to unsolicited marketing because you know what your training requirements are. Selecting the right vendor starts with deciding if the vendor is offering training which would satisfy your needs. This puts you in a much better position than if you don't know what you need.

If you have built a good development plan, you won't have to react to marketing at all. You will be searching out the training you need before you receive the periodic advertisement.

So, I recommend you follow my wife's advice on selecting your vendors:

1. Review any evaluations you can get from internal customers. Has anyone in your organization taken this course from the vendor?
2. Has anyone in your organization taken any courses from this vendor?
3. Can you get reviews by other customers? Are these reviews published?
4. Can you get a list of references from the vendor?

When you find someone to ask, you need to ensure you ask the right question. You're not looking for the last 3-5 years of customer satisfaction survey results. These are not reliable indicators of the effectiveness of the training. You don't want to know if the attendees found the instructor captivating. You don't want to know if the customers rated the course 4.8 out of 5. You want the answer to a simple question; "Did the training improve the ability of the student to do the task?"

---

*Did the training improve the ability of the student
to do the task?*

You won't find this question on a customer satisfaction survey, especially on a survey administered at the end of the course. This is why you'll need to narrow your reference pool. Try asking some differentiators:

1. Find a previous customer who does the same job or fills the same role as your worker.

        a. Better is to find someone who performs the same task.
        b. If you can't find a task match, go with role.

2. Ask the previous customer how well they performed the task before training.
        a. Use the scale you evaluated your requirements with.
        b. You need to find as close a match as possible to the task and the level of skill before the training.

3. Ask the customer how well they were able to perform after the training.
        a. It's great if you can ask if training was the reason for the improvement.

Basically, you want to know if the training was worth the cost. Unfortunately, most previous customers won't be able to tell you the answer. Even if they know what tasks they want training on, and understand the processes involved, most don't take the time to evaluate the effectiveness of the training.

But, don't settle. You want confidence that the training will actually help to make your worker's better. You want offerings that will increase the skill-level of those performing the task. This is a question I rarely hear asked by the worker, the supervisor, or even the vendor. How many times have you been asked by a vendor if the training you completed a few months ago was effective? You can't ask this during the training or immediately afterward. You have to ask this after the customer has had time to apply the training.

So what's the best way to select the training you want? Find others who have taken it and see if it did what it was supposed to – that's improve the skill of those who attended.

Chapter 2-7
Scheduling, assessing, and tracking training

If you are going to use formal training or a vendor for any of your training you'll need to decide if you will bring the instructor on site or if the trainees will have to travel. In either case you will have to check on availability of the instructor or course.

When you've figured all of this into your plan, you will actually schedule the training. You can do so based on the priorities you determined for each gap; balanced with the availability, cost, and length of the training.

This part isn't hard and shouldn't warrant more than a single line on a to-do list. But, this simple step is where most managers fall off the path. Here are the common mistakes managers make with scheduling:

1. *Mistake*: Many managers look to the employees to schedule their own training.
   Why it's a problem: Looks like the manager has abdicated her responsibility.
2. *Mistake*: Managers only schedule the next month's training instead of 6-12 months out.
   Why it's a problem: It makes it hard for long range planning. It also communicates that it's not important enough to schedule further out, as if there's no future.
3. *Mistake*: Managers don't help clear the employee's schedule to ensure they are ready and able to attend.
   Why it's a problem: If the training is important, and of course it is, the manager should actively help to clear the worker's calendar.
4. *Mistake*: Managers don't budget for the training.

Why it's a problem: you really don't need me to tell you why this is a problem, do you?

This is no time for the manager to abdicate. Up until this step the manager and worker have been building a strong, collaborative relationship, leveraging all of the opportunities for conversations around the position, the tasks, and the training. Here is where the manager gets to close the deal. The manager has built up some equity with the worker...and if the manager doesn't close the deal, all of that effort could be lost. If you want to prove to your worker that you care about him, than you need to stay motivated and focused. If you can follow through here you will finish winning your workers over.

1. Budget for the training to make sure you have the funds needed.
2. Help the worker find the right day and times to receive the training, especially when it's self-paced.
3. Help the worker actually sign up for and schedule the training.
4. Discuss the expectations for the training well before the date.
5. After the training, ask the employee how it went.
6. Review the development plan to see if the gap is spanned or if additional training is necessary.
7. Don't quit until the employee is fully trained.

Bottom line? If the workers are the organization's greatest assets, then treat them as such. Developing an employee has to be one of the manager's top priorities and most important responsibilities to the organization. So, schedule the training. Plan for it and put it in the calendar. If you have an organizational calendaring tool use it so everyone knows that the worker will be unavailable and that you value her development enough to not only put funding on the line, but also other work. Time is truly our greatest commodity, so invest it in the worker's development.

When you schedule the training, with the worker, remind her that it's not a vacation. In the Air Force we'd call some training opportunities "boondoggles." These aren't truly training opportunities – they're actually paid vacations. A bad conference quickly becomes a boondoggle. Avoid it. You have expectations for your worker. You want them to not only attend, you need them to learn.

Besides being extremely picky about the sources for your training, even when selecting an in-house trainer, you also want to ensure that the training will deliver what you need.

You probably guessed it…the MTL will once again give you what you need. Good vendors, instructors, and course materials should have criterion referenced objectives (CROs) for each training session. A criterion referenced objective has the format, "given ___ the trainee will be able to _____ at a ____ level." Basically it's what you will receive, what you'll be able to do as a result, and to what skill level. These are a staple of an Air Force training offering, but is rare in the corporate or higher education worlds. The criterion referenced objective works best for practical training…or, dare I say it, *tasks*.

Here is an example; "*Given* 3 hours of training on pivot tables *the trainee will be able to* create a pivot table with the needed filters and calculated fields *as* prescribed in the syllabus."

Yes, even software applications can be taught using a CRO. But if you aren't lucky enough to have these predefined in the marketing materials for the course offering you still have your MTL. Don't hesitate to ask the vendor or the in-house expert, if the training will cover the tasks you need.

Using the same example from the CRO for pivot tables the tasks would look like:

- Identify source data; worksheet, table, or range.
- Determine data readiness for pivot; is there a primary key? Are the data types consistent throughout each field?
- Modify data as needed to make pivot-ready.
- Create pivot table from data source.
- Test validity of pivot table.
- Create filters.
- Create slicers.
- Create calculated fields.

As someone who loves to teach, I would be excited to have a potential client offer this list. As an instructor, I always want to give the students what they need. The best feeling in the world is teaching a skill and knowing that the student gets it. How awesome would it be to know walking in exactly what the student needs to learn?

Even if you don't have a task breakdown, if you identify higher level tasks (create pivot table with filters and calculated fields), you will have a higher level of confidence that you'll get what you need. If you provide the higher level tasks – ask the vendor for a task breakdown. They should definitely be able to give you the lower-level tasks which go into the process they are training.

This is why one of the sources for task breakdowns can be training offerings.

Whatever you do, schedule the training as seriously as you schedule the most important meetings you have. Don't let the training take second place to other priorities...it's the quickest way to convince the organization that developing the staff is not actually important. When you schedule it, make that time untouchable and then ensure the worker knows that when he is attending the training he is still working. You are paying him for his time, just as if he were at his desk. Actually you're spending more on him than normal as you're likely paying for the training on top of his salary. And if the training is off-site, you're likely paying for his travel and lodging also.

Assessing training

Most managers think that their only responsibility is to ensure that the worker actually attended the training. But that's not going to ensure that you get a proper return on your investment. The next step is to evaluate the effectiveness of the training. This is a critical step which most managers totally miss. You have to evaluate the training.

You have to ask yourself, "Was the training worth the expense?" Even in-house training has a cost. External training usually comes with a high price tag especially if you add in travel and lodging and then the time away from the job. Make sure you get your money's worth. The best way to determine the value you received is to assess the effectiveness of the training.

Being a good steward of organizational resources requires that you be concerned with the value received for the investment and how effective the training was may be the most important area to assess. The good news is that you have a tool for measuring the benefits received. We go back to the development plan and we step through the skill assessment process. We are trying to determine how far the needle moved. How much improved is the worker's performance? Just as before, we'll make this determination as a team – using both the worker's input and observation. Did the worker think it was worthwhile? This is yet another opportunity for a conversation. Remember during your conversation that the results are *not* the only consideration.

This will not only give you a good read on how effective the training was but you'll also have a clear picture of the gap. Has it lessened? Has it disappeared? Or will more training be required?

Besides determining how much better the worker can perform the tasks covered you can also ask:

1. Should you use the training for others who need it or find a different source?
2. Did the training cover unneeded items? If so, can the training be tailored for your needs?
3. Did the worker attain enough of a skill level to allow him to teach others what he learned? At a minimum, can the worker give a presentation of what he learned?

Remember, when you reassess the worker's performance, it is first a reflection on the training, and only later will you discuss how it can be a reflection on the worker.

Track progress against the plan

The development plan has to be a *living* plan. The manager and worker have to review it, use it for conversation, and fully collaborate on the fulfillment of the plan. It is a tool for improvement – improvement of the worker's performance, improvement of the relationship between the manager and worker, and improvement of the organization's culture and climate. Use the tool regularly to be successful.

The development plan has to be a living plan,
it's a tool for improvement.

Make notes in the margin. One of the best proofs of how good a plan is, is if it is used. Not how much it is read or how well it is written – the best test is how much it is used. There should be notes handwritten on the plan. Notes about the training tried, the progress made, and next steps. The development plan doesn't need to be a clean product.

Let no dust settle on the plan!

Don't make this an annual exercise. If you have regular one-on-one sessions, make the training plan a tool you use every time. Unless, and until, the worker is fully skilled, keep using the plan – annual goals should always include development objectives.

Use the plan. Use it as a discussion tool, use it to document training used, and use it to track the effectiveness of the training.

Hopefully by this time both of you are sold on the plan's benefits. Once the worker is fully skilled you will start using it for the continued growth of your staff. Development need not stop upon full skill attainment.

Any living development plan should include these components:

- Master Task List
- Training requirement position analysis
- Individual evaluation
- Tracking of training selected
- Evaluation of training used

If you've followed along and used this book as a guide, you should have all of the artifacts listed above. You can download free examples of Microsoft Excel ® templates I've made for these at my website, mkknowledgebuilders.com.

Recurring training

I keep using sports, and especially professional sports, in my analogies because like the military, sports provide a great example of professional development done right. For any team to excel and reach their full potential, all members of the team have to continuously seek to develop their skills.

An amateur athlete's training doesn't stop when they reach the pro ranks – it actually increases. Most sports even have an exhibition season to prepare for the real day to day work of the regular season. Baseball's spring training is legendary for developing the player and the team as a cohesive unit.

How I wish the corporate world would have the same focus on development. Of course there are the exceptions, the organizations that do have this focus. They unfortunately are the rare case instead of the norm.

Some skills require practice and periodic maintenance to ensure the worker will continue to perform at a high level. In the military some prime examples are pilots. They constantly train for the time when they will have to use their skills in life and death situations. Fire fighters, first responders, and emergency room doctors do the same. There are many jobs where the sports mentality can be found. But it's rare to find it in an environment where the workers don't have emergency care or life and death scenarios to deal with. We expect this from the military, those who protect and serve, and our medical professions. But this is also evident with trial lawyers, inspectors, and the best restaurants. The question isn't why it exists in a few non-critical professions…the question is why doesn't it exist in all professions?

Sports makes sense because you are paid for performance and the performance evaluation is public, transparent, and immediate. Oh that all jobs had such obvious measures of success.

Note that I am not suggesting that you make the required skill level a "moving target." This is a horrible way to create annual goals and it's an equally horrible way to develop your staff. Even in sports there is a minimum standard required to make the team. And then there is a "below the line" goal for continuous improvement. The very best players of any age, in any sport, continuously push themselves to improve. To become the very best they can be.

It is a personality trait more than a learned behavior – a desire to reach personal perfection. It is this drive more than anything else which separates the legendary from the ordinary. So, don't be surprised if your workforce lacks this trait. But also, if you find even a little of this desire in your people, feed it, support it, and help it flourish.

While it is not common in any field of endeavor, it's not as rare as you may think. And if personal improvement is even a small desire in your worker you can help to fertilize it so that it grows naturally.

You don't have to be an athlete to want to be
the best at whatever you do.

I've covered this before, but it is worth repeating. You have a couple of chances to get workers who have a desire to improve themselves. You can and should hire with this desire as a major determining factor in your selection process. Especially now that you've made it to this point in the book, you should be confident that you can train on the tasks required to do the job. You need not hire the person who is the most skilled or the most qualified to do the job. Instead you should hire based on who will fit your organization the best. Who will be a good team player on your particular team. A hire who truly seeks to grow and improve. Someone's whose values fit your organizations.

Or you could hire based on skill sets. You could hire with the outlook that you can save training dollars by hiring the most skilled worker. And if his personality, attitude or values are off-center from your organization's you can always change him...

Paragraph breaks indicate a pause. Ellipses (three consecutive periods) also indicates a pause. I am pausing because I can't stop from laughing at the picture of you actually believing you could change a person for less cost than train them to perform a task. Of course my publisher will chastise me for laughing at a reader – but I know "that guy" isn't you. Right?

You may need to schedule recurring training differently. It may be necessary by regulation to have periodic updates to certifications. If the skill level of the worker doesn't oscillate in-between training sessions, feel free to simply schedule this training as you would an annual doctor's appointment. You don't need it in the development plan although you may want to track certifications in a separate worksheet and mark it with the dates of the last certification so the worker has this if needed.

> *"If a man is called to be a street sweeper, he should sweep streets even as a Michelangelo painted, or Beethoven composed music or Shakespeare wrote poetry. He should sweep streets so well that all the hosts of heaven and earth will pause to say, 'Here lived a great street sweeper who did his job well."*
>
> *~ Martin Luther King Jr.*

Plan templates

The abbreviation PDP can stand for more than professional development plan. It can also be a positional development plan – the plan which captures the required tasks and skills for a given job. PDP can also stand for personal development plan – when you take the positional version and apply it to an individual. Seems confusing? No worries as it really doesn't matter what you call it – they are all versions of the same plan. You can also go the other direction and create a development plan for a functional area. It's all based on the tasks you analyze. Each functional area can have a master MTL that can be broken down into multiple positional versions.

Training requirements can be classified further if it makes planning easier. Some suggested classifications are: Job qualification tasks, professional development tasks, ancillary tasks, and additional training tasks.

A sample template for a development plan follows. It was developed in Excel ® and includes a visual mapping of the skill level. It also includes a way to track skill and knowledge level evaluations and goals. One sheet is for training evaluation, the other is for scheduling and tracking training received.

Training	Date Schedule	Date Complete	Source	Tasks	skill lvl before trng	Req'd	Skill lvl after	% Trained	Priority
Basic Course - B001PMI	1/1/2014	1/3/2014	PMI	Conduct Initial needs assessment	2.5	3.5	3	86%	C
Basic Course - B001PMI				Promote project request to proposed status	3	4	4	100%	C
Basic Course - B001PMI				Execute completed plan/design	3	4.3	3.25	76%	B
Basic Course - B001PMI				Meet and work with customers to develop detailed requirements	3.25	4	3.5	88%	A
Intermediate Course - C002PMI	3/2/2014	3/5/2014	PMI	Conduct Initial needs assessment	3	3.5	3.75	107%	C
Intermediate Course - C002PMI				Execute completed plan/design	3.25	4.3		76%	B
Intermediate Course - C002PMI				Meet and work with customers to develop detailed requirements	3.5	4		88%	A
Intermediate Course - C002PMI				Finalize design and present to the design review committee	3	4		75%	C
Intermediate Course - C002PMI				Complete closeout process	3.5	3.7		95%	B
Intermediate Course - C002PMI				Walk Project Manager/Relationship Manager through planning process	3.5	3.7		95%	B
Intermediate Course - C002PMI				Walk Project Manager/Relationship Manager through execution process	3	4		75%	B
Intermediate Course - C002PMI				Walk Project Manager/Relationship Manager through closeout process	3	3.8		79%	B

Figure 1, for tracking status of training scheduled/received

Task	Skill Level			Training Schedule				% trained
	Now	Req't	Priority	Proj start date	Actual St Date	Proj end date	Actual End date	80%
Area 1								
Walk Project Manger/Relationship Manager through Request creation process	3	4	A					75%
Consult on readiness to promote project request to proposed status	2.5	3.8	B					66%
Walk Project Manager/Relationship Manager through planning process	3.5	3.7	B					95%
Walk Project Manager/Relationship Manager through design process	3	3	B					100%
Walk Project Manager/Relationship Manager through execution process	3	4	B					75%
Walk Project Manager/Relationship Manager through closeout process	3	3.8	B					79%
Conduct Initial needs assessment	2.5	3.5	C					71%
Submit the project request to review process	2.75	3.5	C					79%
Promote project request to proposed status	3	4	C					75%
Meet and work with customers to develop detailed requirements	3.25	4	A					81%
Finalize design and present to the design review committee	3	4	C					75%

Figure 2, for evaluating skill/knowledge level

For examples of filling these forms out, see the practicum section. These are only examples. You don't have to use these templates or any pre-made tools. You can create your own in any tool you like, including a notebook and pen. The plan is only as good as the amount of use it gets. It doesn't have to be pretty. It definitely doesn't need to be in a three-ring binder with a glossy cover. It needs to be used.

So, take these templates only as a sample.

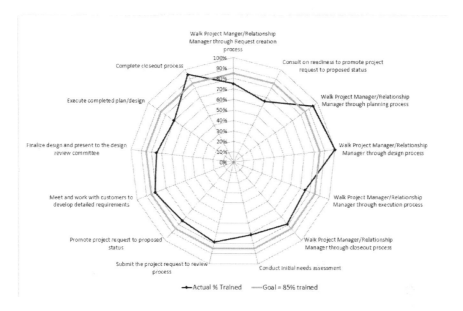

Figure 3, sample of a chart for analysis of training evaluation

The spider web chart above can give a quick feel for how well the worker is doing towards achieving the required skill level for specific task groups or tasks. The idea behind any chart or graph should be to simplify the message and make it easier for the user to understand the story. Hopefully that means I don't have to spend a lot of time or space explaining the chart.

The black line shows where the worker currently is – follow the lines, threads of the web, from the task to the black marker. The grey line is where you want the worker to be.

Chapter 2-8
Benefiting from the information

There are some not-so-obvious benefits you will gain from using professional development plans. I'll cover five important extra-benefits, but you will probably find others without too much difficulty.

Succession planning

An important leadership concern which has reappeared on the horizon is the need to find successors for the key leadership positions within the organization. Roles such as the Chief Executive Officer, Chief Information Officer, Chief Finance Officer, Executive Director, and Operations Director benefit greatly from having "hand-picked" and personally groomed successors. Sometimes these successors are from outside organizations. Sometimes they are developed from the day they are hired. While this concept seems logical, personally I haven't seen it effectively put into action yet.

That may be partly because the process for preparing the successor for the position is rarely planned. If each position, even the top levels have professional development plans then grooming a replacement for a position becomes easier. The projected successor's capabilities would be assessed, and then a clear plan would be put in place. In the case of leadership positions, much of the training may be satisfied through coaching and mentoring.

You can learn a ton from sports teams in this area. High School teams develop replacements for all positions, colleges recruit and then develop replacements, and even pro teams draft and develop for their succession plans. Businesses seem to ignore this need. Perhaps it's because organizations are overly optimistic about having their best workers stay with the company. This is actually a pretty short-sighted way of thinking. There are so many reasons you may lose your brightest and best that not having a succession plan is irresponsible.

Succession plans for key positions on a sports team aren't restricted to the players. Most good teams also have plans for developing coaches. Think about the teams that replace their coaches internally. They seem to keep the ball rolling without any loss in quality or momentum. This is an example of a solid program and a good coaching staff. When the coaches are *fired* the parent organization looks to start fresh and doesn't want to replace from within. As a Notre Dame fan I've watched this play out for a long time. It seemed like every couple of years the University had to go out shopping for the *right* coach. And you look at schools like Stanford which replaced Coach Harbough with Coach Shaw…an internal replacement. The same happens in the pros. Bobby Bayliss, the Notre Dame Men's Tennis coach for 26 years developed his replacement, Ryan Sachire.

Sometimes organizations want to shop from outside to get a fresh perspective. I think there's definite benefits from getting other perspectives. I'm just not sure that you want that as your main criteria for hiring into your key positions.

One way around this is to include external possibilities in your succession plan – but externals who were previously workers in your organization. Many teams bring back ex-players or assistant coaches who have been gaining experience at other organizations. This is what happened with Ryan Sachire. He was a player with Notre Dame (the number one position) and after having a respectable professional career was an assistant coach at Baylor University. This is one of the best reasons to develop your people, even when it means they may leave for other opportunities. Since you were a major player in their development and they left on good terms – you have a larger pool for your succession plan.

You don't need to have a complicated succession plan for every position, but you should have an idea how you would replace any of your key players. It shouldn't be a new adventure if it becomes necessary. Instead it should be a journey you've thought about.

If you have development plans for all of your positions or at least key positions, you will be able to identify which positions should have succession plans. You'll also have a much easier time of implementing those succession plans.

Cross-training

Another popular concept which is rarely fulfilled is cross-training. The concept is a good one – training workers to be able to fill more than one role so there is coverage when someone is unavailable. It also makes attacking problems easier as you have more skilled hands available in a crisis.

Cross-training also helps everyone to understand the big-picture of what the organization is working on. Project teams are easier to form when the make-up of the team is less restricted because you only have a few workers with the right set of skills. It is a *force-multiplier*. Single-threaded skills put the organization at risk. It also makes for a stressful environment for the person filling the position.

The funny thing is, cross-training tends to threaten those who are in the single-threaded positions. Most will resist this sharing of responsibilities and skills. This is an immature behavior within the company brought about because you have failed to create a team atmosphere. Once again sports teach us a great lesson here. Although any quarterback on any team wants to be *the man*, every player also wants the team to win more than they want to start. Imagine a team with only one quarterback or one field goal kicker. What would happen if that player was no longer available?

This is where I think we've gone pitifully wrong in our fear of developing competition in our children. A competitive nature is a healthy thing. In the Air Force, one of our mantras was "Officers Compete." We want our players to compete to make it onto the field. We want three players, if possible, competing for each position. The current starter may feel like his status is threatened...but rather than resist the efforts of the organization to develop others in the position, we want the starter to be challenged and pushed to excel. We can't afford for the quarterback's self-worth to be tied to being the only one who can perform the duties. Instead it has to be tied to being the best.

In businesses I find many times the single-threaded position holder feels threatened if anyone is cross-trained into his responsibilities. This attitude and fear has to be overcome because the best person to assist in the cross-training is the person currently doing the job. We have to change our focus from the individual to the team. We have to change our self-worth from being the *only* skilled person for a given position to being the *most* skilled person.

So many things become broken when you are single-threaded. Not only do you perpetuate the individual-focus over team but you also encourage the person holding that position to have an unhealthy work-life balance. The single-threaded person finds he can't take vacations like others. The single-threaded person has to take their work home with them. Even though this makes the worker feel good about himself and gives him a sense of job security – it creates a very stressful work life. This same person will work against efforts to cross-train others into his position while becoming more and more stressed because of being the only one who can do his job. He'll complain to his family that he has to work while on vacation, but then circumvent efforts to share his duties. If this sounds like dysfunctional behavior...I've described it accurately.

You have to do more than implement cross-training. You will have to deal with change management issues for all involved, unless you have built a team culture. I may sound like a broken record, but all of the organizational development tools (Development Plans, Metrics, Strategic Planning, Open Communications, Project Management, Process Management, Internal Assessments, Process Asset Libraries, and Service Level Agreements) require the organization NOT be suffering from Organizational Immaturity. See "Why Organizations Struggle So Hard to Improve So Little: Overcoming Organizational Immaturity" for more information on why this happens.

If you have professional development plans for each position and your organization is ready, you can pick and choose which tasks to cross-train versus trying to train a complete position. You can identify coaches and mentors from the skill evaluations and match the right workers together. Cross-training can make your team powerful, allowing for coverage, better skill development, and better project teams.

Expanding skill sets

In many fields, required skills sets for a given position keep changing. Normally expanding, sometimes contracting. Information Technology is a great example of a field in which skill sets keep changing. New software applications, new technologies, and modifications to existing systems almost ensures that the skills for a given position will change as will the required level of performance. The living development plan is made to expand along with the job requirements. Rather than knee-jerk reactions to new tasks, the manager and worker can calmly add tasks to the MTL and run the process, ending with a workable plan.

One way you see this clearly in the corporate world is the fascination with trying to do more with less. One way to do this is through automation. Another is through process improvement.

And another viable means of reaching this goal is giving more tasks to existing positions. This last one requires a change in development plans. You may think this is just cross-training…and it could be. But it would be an expansion if you have eliminated a position and are transitioning the tasks to existing positions. This is a means of saving a salary by not replacing a loss. I don't believe this is especially viable unless the lost position was superfluous to a degree in the first place.

One Associated Press journalist in 2010 claimed that American's returning to the workplace when the economy started to turn around, found themselves *unqualified* for their old positions and therefore couldn't get the job. This was supposedly due to the expansion of job descriptions during the downturn. I can buy the idea that positions were expanded. What I don't buy is that the same organizations that reportedly expanded the responsibilities of a given position would then expect that they could hire people with these new mixed skills to fill this new hybrid position. Logically, you'd hire someone with strong core skills and *if* you wanted to keep the position a hybrid, you'd train internally just as you did when you had to because of necessity.

This actually happens much slower in sports. Think of your favorite sports team. Roles and positions change very slowly. New systems come about slowly. New rules affect the game faster than innovations.

But in business, especially ones involving technology, tasks, processes, and policies change regularly. Rarely is a position description good for more than a year or two.

Peter Weddle posited in an online article, "How the World of Work Has Changed" 2011, (http://www.higheredjobs.com/articles/articleDisplay.cfm?ID=291) that "[Most companies] are engaging in what might best be described as "rapid adaptation. They know they can no longer survive, let alone prosper, by standing still -- by doing what they've always done -- so they are adjusting as rapidly as they can to the changes going on around them. And those adaptations are changing the nature of the work they need done and thus the jobs and kinds of employees they require..."

This seems intuitively true, especially if the job involves technology, which almost all do now. What isn't readily evident is the existence of valid job descriptions, Master Task Listings, or development plans. The more volatile job descriptions are becoming, the more solid development plans are necessary. The best way to keep up with constant change is to plan for it.

Although it is obvious that technology is changing all the time, businesses are woefully negligent in updating position descriptions or MTLs for a given position.

Lateral job changes

On the same line with cross-training, lateral job changes give workers opportunities outside of their current position. Not everyone wants to be promoted or become management. Many workers want to learn more about the business as a whole or to try other areas. Many times feelings of being *stuck in a rut* aren't due to a lack of promotion, but instead a lack of change.

You can use the development plan in multiple ways. You can identify the tasks needed for the lateral move and determine how much training would be required. Remember, many tasks may be common or enough like others that you can leverage existing training. You can use it to set a minimum qualification level in the worker's current position before you allow retraining. You can use the development plans for the new position, providing guidelines on what will be required. The plans for the new position can also help the worker determine if he really wants to make the lateral change. Of course a short stint of job shadowing will also help, but it's nice to be able to hand the worker a comprehensive document outlining the tasks and the requisite performance levels for those tasks.

Hiring with the intent to train

Perhaps the most amazing thing I've found about professional development plans and hiring practices is that there rarely are any development plans in place before a person is hired. And when they are, they aren't used in the hiring process. What is amazing is the proclivity of managers to try to hire people who are fully skilled in the given position (I lamented this in the section on expanding skill sets). This is great if you are offering a commensurate salary, but most times you try to hire someone for less than a fully qualified worker would warrant. With a development plan in hand, you can hire based on attitude, cultural fit, and willingness to learn. You can hire a person you'd *like* to work with, someone who will fit in. Someone who will want to come to work every day. By not letting the lack of ability in a specific task stop you from hiring her, you broaden the pool of possible candidates.

When you have a good plan in place, you know how long it will take and how much it will cost to fill in the gaps in ability. It is so freeing to know that you can hire based on potential and fit instead of the normal litany of "experience in, expertise in, skills, and knowledge." After the improved inter-personal relationships, hiring without fear of deficiencies may be the greatest benefit from having positional development plans.

This is an essential and foundational benefit of having development plans in place. You can stop trying to be objective in your hiring process and start being fully subjective. This may seem oxymoronic to you (or just moronic). But, I assure you, I want you to be more subjective and less objective in hiring your next worker.

*You should be more subjective and less objective
when hiring.*

Why? Because you're not hiring a machine. You're not selecting a software application or a piece of hardware. You're not selecting a vendor. There is no Request For Proposal and the need to have three independent bids. You are hiring a new worker. You are looking for a new family member – and you can't do this through formulas and lists of requirements.

I am always shocked when someone tells me that they removed all subjectivity from their hiring process. They beam with pride when they tell me how they used an objective questionnaire, maybe a skill test, and an objective review of the applicants' resumes to select their hire. They beam with pride and I shudder with fear. These objective selection tools mean that there is no assessment of how well the potential hire will fit within the organization. There is no consideration of how well the new hire will get along with the current team. There is no evaluation of the chemistry or lack thereof, the new hire will have with the organization.

Professional sports teams have learned this lesson the hard way. In the past they drafted players based solely on statistical analysis. This misses the subjective areas of personality, values, and morals. When enough draft choices ended in a bust – not because they couldn't play but because of unevaluated soft things, the scouting process changed. Now teams ask tons of questions, hold interviews, and check with references to find out what type of person the player is. They still use the objective measures to help them find their potential choices, but now they use subjective viewpoints to make their final decision.

If you have a solid development plan in place and confidence in your ability to develop your workers, you can focus on the more important traits for hiring; self-discipline, common values, common morals, self-motivation, self-starter, etc.

Since past performance isn't an accurate indicator of future results, you shouldn't put too much weight into these objective measures. Instead focus on the fit and the potential.

This is why the best college football teams, like Notre Dame, will use the independent ratings, number of stars according to the many organizations that make a business of rating High School players as a starting point, but not the only deciding factor. The best teams look at the player's work ethic, potential for growth, and attitude. The best teams recruit players that fit their system as well as their culture. As Brian Kelly has said when talking about a recruit, "he's the *Right Kinda Guy* (RKG)." I'm sure there'll be a book about Coach Kelly's tenure at some point and that book will include a chapter about recruiting the RKG. For my purposes the key point is that the RKG is more than a good football player – Coach Kelly was looking first for high quality people who wanted a high quality education and to be part of the Notre Dame family. Not just for two or three years, but for a lifetime. To quote one of those recruits, "…they're recruiting guys who are great players, but even better people."

Why should your organization seek anything less?

One of the factors that naturally get calculated into the equation is the player's choice. They have to want to come to your team. Unlike the job market, these best players normally receive multiple offers from high quality teams; the better the player, the more offers. So the player has to want to play for the team, he has to want to join your team. This helps in a natural selection process.

This also exemplifies why potential hires should do the same. A valuable hire should cultivate multiple offers from different organizations and then choose the one he thinks he'll fit in.

Training database

As you produce more development plans, you'll have more and more useful information. You'll have a list of training sources, internal and external, with evaluations of their effectiveness in training specific tasks. This information can be used to fulfill other training needs across the organization. You'll also have good data on the effectiveness of the different methods you've tried for each task.

In-house training

Since you've assessed the internal trainers, you know which are good at it and which aren't. You can leverage the in-house experts in a classic win-win situation. Not only do you get affordable training for your workforce, but one of the best ways to recognize your staff is to recognize their expertise. As this progresses, you find that you actually build a culture of learning. Instead of silos and hoarding of information, you promote sharing of knowledge and an organizational view of the world. When workers think of "us vs. them" the "*us*" changes from the *workers* to the *organization* and the "*them*" changes from *management* to the *competition*. Of course professional development plans won't make this happen all by themselves...but it's a great start in the right direction.

Skills database

Along with information on the training sources and methods you've tried, you also have a very valuable database of the tasks which make up the positions in the organization, the performance levels required for each, and the skill levels of each employee. This information can be stored in a skills database. With this information you can visualize the organization in a new light – as a structure made up of different talents and abilities. Leadership's perception of what the organization is capable of changes and grows with the realization of the skills within it. All of the benefits listed become easier to realize when you have a complete picture of the organization's skills and abilities. Granted this will take some time. In "Why Organizations Struggle So Hard to Improve So Little: Overcoming Organizational Immaturity" we explained the high likelihood of failure if you attempt to implement any improvement effort enterprise-wide, and using professional development plans is no exception. It will take time…time and persistence. But if you get the managers that already believe in developing their people to participate, soon you'll have a start, the basis for your databases. As more come on board you will add to the structure you had the foresight to construct. As the organization and individual managers start to reap the benefits, more will participate and your information store will grow.

Professional development planning and the "Toyota Way"

The "Toyota Way" – like most good concepts and principles for getting things done, has to be adhered to in good times and bad for it to be effective. Quality Management, Total Quality Management, the Capability Maturity Model, and the Toyota Way are just a few examples of excellent systems for raising the level of any organization.

My first book, written with Michael Langthorne and Don Padgett, delves into why organizations which try to adopt any of these proven methods fail to see the same levels of success. The philosophies are not at fault. They work. They make sense.

I haven't met anyone who looks at any of these methods and says, "that'll never work" or "nah, the way we do it today is better." One thing all of these systems have in common is the need to develop personnel. There is the obligatory training in the system itself, but every one of them relies on the development of staff. The Toyota Way for example relies heavily on internal development of staff and leadership.

And unfortunately when an organization working within one of these systems falls from grace by losing its focus – one of the first things that falls by the wayside is personnel development. New leadership decides they don't need the training. Existing personnel decide that they've "got it" and avoid any continual development.

The organization tries to hire people who have already worked in the same Organizational Development model – so they won't have to train them. This is seriously broken thinking because the training is not a supplementary consideration – it's a primary criteria for success.

Chapter 2-9
Bonus Material

Why resistance?

Believe it or not, a fair amount of people (managers and leadership) believe that if they train their workers to be the best they can be, bad things will happen. I don't know if this is borne of experience or ignorance, but it can derail a champion's efforts to implement development plans.

The normal misconceptions and incorrect beliefs include:

    a. "We'll lose them to our competitors"
    b. "They'll be overqualified"
    c. "They'll want a raise"
    d. "They'll want a promotion"
    e. "We can't afford to train them"
    f. "Training is a waste of time – if they wanted to do better, they would"

I share these ridiculous errors in thinking because you may find yourself battling against them. It's not hard to explain why they are misguided, but if you don't expect the resistance, you may lose some ground dealing with your shock. That's the thing about organizational improvement…the champions of change think the need for the change is so obvious that they are shocked when they run into opposition.

This shock can give the enemies of change a temporary advantage. Temporary because eventually the "right will win out" but you don't want to waste time with having to overcome the initial loss of ground. So, be prepared for the resistance. Be prepared and calmly explain the benefits (pick from the ones listed here) and if you feel compelled to do so, explain why each misconception is off base.

As with most ignorance, these misconceptions are rooted in fear. Mostly a fear of loss; loss of power, loss of control, loss of revenue, and loss of status. In reality the organization and the leader who promotes learning will gain in all of these areas. When you can show the naysayers the truth of these statements you'll win them over.

Power

Everyone will gain in self-worth and personal power. When you train others, you become better yourselves. When I want to help a player become better at a position, I have her train someone else (usually a rookie). Invariably she becomes better because her focus becomes laser sharp. Also her self-esteem rises as she knows I trust her to teach another. Finally, you move from the false feelings of power due to hording knowledge and move toward real feelings of power awarded to those who become valuable players on the team by helping others develop.

Control

Control like power is usually a false feeling taken, not earned. When you horde knowledge and feel that you have job security because you are the only ones who can perform certain tasks…you live a lie. You have no control in these cases. Instead, you are locked in a rut of your own design. Real control comes from the ability to change. Real control comes from flexibility. And to gain this control you have to embrace a culture of learning and development. You not only want others to be the best they can be, you seek this level of excellence for yourselves.

Imagine a basketball team where the star player doesn't want any of the other players to improve because they may become the "star." Or one where the star doesn't want to improve her game. Again I turn to the benefits of healthy competition. Officers Compete. Athletes Compete. Winners Compete. This doesn't mean you should blindly compete and disdain collaboration. Just the opposite. To truly compete means to push yourself and others to be the best.

Revenue

This may be the strangest misbelief. When you develop your people, they become more confident. They expand their capabilities and improve their performance. With training you can truly do more with less. If you want to be competitive in today's market you have to get better. You have to continuously improve – not just processes, but also individual performance. You won't lose revenue. Money spent on developing personnel is the best investment you can make. You get the best return for your dollar – especially when you consider the different types (in-house, self-paced, etc.) of training available.

Status

This one is hard to argue against. If you find your self-worth in hording information and being the only one who can perform a task…it's hard to say that you will be better off if others are as good as you. If you equate your personal status at work with being single-threaded and not being knowledgeable of other areas, I don't really have much for you. Except that I truly believe your organization will be better off without you.

Seriously.

I'd recommend they let you go. I'd much rather have someone who realizes it's a choice between what's best for the organization and what's best for the individual. I want a team player. I want someone who wants to learn, to progress, to develop. I want someone who doesn't need to be the only one who knows how to perform a task to feel they are valued by the organization.

That said, if the organization is the one which is creating this culture – I truly believe the worker would be better off in a different organization. I'd recommend you leave the organization.

In my experience it's a blend of both – the organization promotes this broken thinking and the individual happily lives within what the organization has created. You do this every time you reward firefighting, when you applaud the worker who cuts his vacation short to come in and solve a crisis, and when you fail to develop others.

The bottom line is that if the organization is suffering from Organizational Immaturity, it will have a hard time fully implementing professional development plans. As explained in our book on the topic, as a champion, you can reap most of the benefits for your unit without having the entire organization adopt it. And if you are in one of these organizations, that's the best you can do. But, if you are blessed and are in an organization which is mature enough to implement Development Plans across the board, the benefits will grow exponentially. This is truly one of the most powerful Organizational Development tools out there.

What about recurring training?

An exception to the "normal" Development Plan I presented to you is the case of recurring training. When you know that a skill needs periodic retraining or refresher training, you will run through the same process over and over again. You will have to evaluate the current capabilities of the worker, then schedule, attain, and evaluate training, and reevaluate the worker's abilities. This can occur when the tools of the job change regularly. Updates to software happen more frequently than hardware, but either may trigger the need for more training.

Sometimes you may only need to update the worker on regularly changing rules, policies, or regulations. This happens when ruling bodies (government for example) periodically make changes to different regulations or policies which you have to comply with. You may choose not to consider this "training," but instead schedule recurring reviews of the regulatory documentation.

A good reason to segregate this type of periodic "update" from your Positional Development Plan, especially when it is a certification requirement, is that the overall "percentage trained" would change each time the retraining is scheduled. This may give the wrong message – that during the retraining period that the worker is less qualified than he "should" be. Then again, this may be a useful way to focus the organization on these retraining requirements. Either way works. You just have to decide what works best for you and your organization.

Regardless if you include this in your Development Plan, you will need to account for this type of training need.

Just keep this in mind when you are scheduling training. I would look to separate the recurring items from the rest of the plan. Perhaps list the task and the evaluations of it under the initial plan area (John achieved a 4 skill level in C programming) and then have it also show up on the section for recurring. That way you know that the worker achieved the required skill initially, and then you can track the need for refresher or recurring training as needed.

Soft skills

The area most people have difficulty with (applying this process to) are the soft skills like advising, consulting, assisting, coaching, or mentoring. Other problem tasks include; communicate, mediate, collaborate, and moderate. Sometimes these are the actual task that the worker needs to perform. If the worker's responsibilities include consulting or advising for example, this may be THE task. Other times, advising or consulting are only part of the process to the task…the job doesn't make them "advisors" or "consultants." Like "advising leadership on the best choices for…" the task may actually be "make recommendations on…" and the "advising" is just a description of how to carry out the task.

The goal is always to get to the "task" – the "what" that actually matters. The way of achieving this goal is to keep "digging" until you get to the underlying tasks. As I covered in the task breakdown, keep going until you actually get to the root task. This will help you determine if the task is a "soft" skill task or not. If it is, you will be able to go about the business of analyzing it without a problem. You get caught up with these tasks because you find it harder to evaluate or describe them.

It may take a little more creativity to measure things like "being creative." But it's far from impossible. Interestingly enough, these soft tasks may require retraining more than the harder more concrete tasks. Keeping up the soft skills requires practice, and unlike the hard tasks (building this, fixing that) there are less observable performances. There are usually tons of data available about how well the hard tasks are being performed. There are usually little to no data available on the performance level of the soft tasks.

Chapter 2-10
RECAP

Creating the Professional Development Plan

In my over twenty years working within the organizational development field, I find that everything remains the same except the name. It seems to be the norm for experts to resurrect past concepts and philosophies, renaming them for the present generation. I worked through Quality, Quality Management, Total Quality Management, Continuous Process Improvement, and Lean Six Sigma. All of these were more alike than different.

When I first learned about creating Development Plans it was in my position as a training specialist for the United States Air Force. The Air Force used Master Task Listings for every Air Force Specialty Code (job) which included insanely thorough task breakdowns. Every task performed for a given job was broken down to the lowest possible level, sounding something like, "turn bolt three quarter turns counter clockwise." This made for training documentation thicker than most large city phone books. From firsthand experience I can attest that most were not utilized in the way intended – it was too much detail and too much to evaluate, review, or use.

I've never forgotten those roots. I've applied what I've learned since those early experiences, tested, tried, and improved the tools for creating Development Plans. At a recent conference I presented a seminar on how to do just this.

The Development Plan is one of the best tools out there you can use to improve your business. You will find the following benefits:

1. Excellent communications between managers and their direct reports.

2. A clear description of what constitutes a given position or role.
3. A practical assessment of each employee's abilities to fulfill their designated role (skills and knowledge).
4. A tool for assessing development solutions.
5. A tool for tracking employee progress against identified position requirements.

A professional development plan is much more than a list of courses, certifications, and vendors. It should (in order):

- Define the position
- Determine how well a given employee fulfills that position
- Identify the gaps in ability and
- Provide a tool for scheduling, tracking, and assessing training to span the gap

You've mined the existing documentation to find a great starting list of tasks for the given position. During the process the manager and worker(s) collaborated.

Remember, after you've finished your document review, you may be missing a lot of tasks. Many times the job has changed multiple times since the documentation was written. Even current job postings have inaccuracies. I've seen job postings which had tasks no longer required and lacking critical tasks the job required.

The manager and worker will need to spend time together to ensure you have a comprehensive list of tasks for the position.

The good news is that the Development Plan will be a living document and easily modified.

The Master Task Listing is as comprehensive a list of tasks as you can pull together. The better job you do on this, the beginning, the easier it will be to create a living plan. The better job you do with the MTL, the better quality of the final plan. Pay your dues up front.

You have captured the tasks out of existing documentation around a given position – this is considered the Positional Master Task Listing. You then built one for each employee. Some employees will have additional duties assigned outside of the position description. These can be anything from organizational development tasks to being an alternate for another worker. When the extra tasks are due to filling in for someone else in their absence, the tasks (and the Development Plans) can be pulled from the primary person's positional plan. For the tasks which are outside of any formal position, you will have to figure out the task list from other sources.

Remember, the manager and employee(s) should perform this process as a team. I highly recommend that the manager and employee rate the position's requirements separately. Then the evaluations of all parties should be compared and discussed. When I facilitate the creation of Development Plans, I collect the evaluations and then bring the parties together to discuss. You spend only a few minutes on any disagreements, with each party giving a very brief explanation of why they scored it the way they did. I usually press for speed because most positions have dozens of tasks. Also because it is less important that the parties come to consensus than that you have a starting point. The simple rule of thumb, if they can't come to consensus within 3 minutes is to go with the highest of the ratings offered. In this case, as with most things, I suggest "Erring on the side of Excellence" and the only harm that will come from having the number higher than it "should be" is that you'll train the workers to be better than necessary (usually a loss of some funds). If you err in the other direction, you could have employees underperforming and unable to complete tasks to the level necessary…and you'd be blaming them for incompetency instead of realizing that you didn't train them to the proper capability level.

You should be proud of yourself... you've now developed a positional Master Task Listing. In so doing you opened new lines of communication with between managers and their direct reports – discussing the tasks that go into the position and how well someone filling the position should be able to accomplish those tasks. The manager and the employee should now have a common understanding of what is expected from the position and the expected level of performance.

This ties in well with Metrics: How to Improve Key Business Results, in which I warn against using "moving targets" to motivate employees' behavior. If you have identified the tasks by position and the expected level of ability associated with each, it is hard to fall into the trap of manipulating behavior. Instead of asking for higher and higher levels of performance, the manager can instead work with the employee to set goals which the employee "owns" and wants to achieve.

If the goals require higher levels of ability than the position called for you need to redefine the job description (and do all of the documentation involved). If the goals require higher levels of ability than your staff currently has, than it is clear that you will need to provide more training to increase their capabilities if they are to have a chance of achieving the goals. Isn't it comforting to know that as a manager you won't expect your workers to perform at a level above their current capabilities – and if you do, that you will provide them with the training to make them successful? I know it's comforting from the employee point of view!

PART THREE
Practicum – Do It Yourself
Development Planning

Chapter 3-1
The Master Task List

Building your Master Task List

As with all processes, creating a professional development plan is made up of steps, prerequisites, inputs, and deliverables (outputs). The first step is to build a Master Task List (MTL) for the position. As a minor review, the only prerequisite to building your MTL is a new position in your organization or an existing position which lacks a development plan.

Time to get your hands dirty. As with a development plan, theory and concepts are good things…but you need to get to the tasks. The same is true for a book on creating development plans. The first task is to build a Master Task List.

The Master Task List is a listing of all tasks that are accomplished by the person filling the position. This is the basis of the development plan. It will be used to identify the minimum job tasks that, when trained, makes a person qualified to do the job. The basis of a good development plan is that all training is based on identified requirements and that all requirements are based on actual tasks. While sources of training may, and frequently do change, the requirement for the training usually does not. The MTL is a listing of the major tasks involved in carrying out a job for a specific position.

Two Rules for Identifying Tasks

Rule 1. Each task has to start with a "verb." Notice that the task break-down above for "create a strategic plan" has five subtasks – each starting with a verb. Regardless of the level you decide to use, each task must start with a verb (or at least have the verb in the task statement somewhere). I don't have to understand the task – but you, and your worker should.

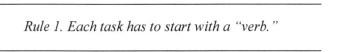

Rule 1. Each task has to start with a "verb."

Rule 2. Each task must actually be a job requirement. Don't put things in the Master Task List for the position which are not actually necessary to the job. It's not a wish list. You will end up using this list to train your worker(s). There is a place for "additional tasks" elsewhere in the plan.

Rule 2. Each task must actually be a job requirement.

Your first task is to research your existing documentation to learn as much as you can about the current role. What tasks make up the position? While you may not be able to look the role up on the internet you can find out a lot about a position.

Normally each position has existing documentation you can start with. You can find out a lot about the position through job descriptions, job postings, past performance evaluations, and process definitions.

Review Existing Documentation

Review existing documentation that may help identify tasks by position. This can include: position descriptions, work schedules, workflow diagrams, and process definitions.

Job Descriptions

One easy to find source for job tasks can be the position or job description. Job descriptions are easy to find because your human resources department will require it when you seek to hire someone for the position. The problem is if you haven't hired for the position recently.

Most managers I've worked with believe they want workers with a specific set of skills and knowledge. This can be a fundamental mistake in perception because it limits not only your ability to find the right hire, but also limits how you go about developing your employees. Using skills and knowledge to define the requirements for a position is inherently vague. Here is an example of a job description for a Human Resources Director.

Human Resources (HR) Director

(from About.com,www.humanresources.about.com/od/jobdescriptions/a/HR_Director_4.htm)

- Above average oral and written communication skills.
- Excellent interpersonal and coaching skills.
- Broad knowledge and experience in employment law, compensation, organizational planning, organization development, employee relations, safety, and training and development.
- Demonstrated ability to lead and develop Human Resources staff members.
- Demonstrated ability to serve as a successful participant on the executive management team that provides company leadership and direction.
- Demonstrated ability to interact effectively with the company Board of Directors.
- Excellent computer skills in a Microsoft Windows environment. Must include Excel and skills in database management and record keeping.
- General knowledge of various employment laws and practices.

- Experience in the administration of benefits and compensation programs and other Human Resources programs.
- Evidence of the practice of a high level of confidentiality.
- Excellent organizational skills.

These may all seem reasonable to have on a job description – and I won't fight that battle here. But, as far as using these as the basis for a development plan, they are woefully insufficient. Of course, if you hire someone who actually fully meets the requirements identified, you might argue that you won't have to train to any of these. Unfortunately, many businesses actually try to find the "dream" hire who actually already has all the skills, knowledge, and abilities required. The simple paradox is that for most positions, the business can't afford to pay what someone would be worth if they fully met the requirements spelled out. No, it's much easier to train someone for most of the job requirements. So, starting with the first item – "oral and written communication skills" – if you gave that to a training specialist to design or purchase training she wouldn't know what to do. And the qualifier of "above average" compounds the vagueness. In Metrics, How To Improve Key Business Results, I stress the importance of super-clarity for requirements. This is another great example where adjectives don't help: "Above average, excellent, broad, general, experience in, and demonstrated ability" will be impossible to measure.

Thankfully, most job descriptions offer skills, knowledge, experience, **and** tasks. You want to focus on the tasks, not the rest of the jargon. It would be hard to build a development plan from the preceding list.

Here's another real life example…

Waiter/Waitress

(from CareerDepot.com http://www.careerdepot.org/Descrip-
tions/job_waiter.htm)

Job Description: Take orders and serve food and beverages to patrons at tables in dining establishment.

- Check patrons' identification in order to ensure that they
  meet minimum age requirements for consumption of alco-
  holic beverages.
- Check with customers to ensure that they are enjoying their
  meals and take action to correct any problems.
- Escort customers to their tables.
- Explain how various menu items are prepared, describing in-
  gredients and cooking methods.
- Inform customers of daily specials.
- Prepare checks that itemize and total meal costs and sales
  taxes.
- Present menus to patrons and answer questions about
  menu items, making recommendations upon request.
- Remove dishes and glasses from tables or counters, and
  take them to kitchen for cleaning.
- Serve food and/or beverages to patrons; prepare and serve
  specialty dishes at tables as required.
- Stock service areas with supplies such as coffee, food, ta-
  bleware, and linens.

This is one of my favorite job descriptions. Every task starts with a
verb. There are a few compounds, but all-in-all I really like the clarity.

You may point out that the job, Waiter/Waitress is more task ori-
ented than an HR Director. You may posit that jobs with a lot of low-

level-tasks and not requiring much creativity or "book learning" might work better for this system than complex jobs. You may even want to argue that complex jobs won't work at all...they're just full of "soft" skills. All I can say in reply is that you'd be wrong. The most complex tasks – pilots of super-complex aircraft and the mainte-nance crew which has to troubleshoot, repair, and maintain the multi-million (billion?) dollar machines can be (and are) broken down into trainable tasks.

Another, more complex example...

Medical Assistant
(from Career Planner.com http://job-descriptions.careerplan-ner.com/Medical-Assistants.cfm)

Perform administrative and certain clinical duties under the direction of physician. Administrative duties may include scheduling appoint-ments, maintaining medical records, billing, and coding for insur-ance purposes. Clinical duties may include taking and recording vi-tal signs and medical histories, preparing patients for examination, drawing blood, and administering medications as directed by physi-cian. Job Duties and Tasks for: "Medical Assistant"

- Interview patients to obtain medical information and measure their vital signs, weight, and height.
- Show patients to examination rooms and prepare them for the physician.
- Record patients' medical history, vital statistics and infor-mation such as test results in medical records.
- Prepare and administer medications as directed by a physi-cian.
- Collect blood, tissue or other laboratory specimens, log the specimens, and prepare them for testing.
- Explain treatment procedures, medications, diets and physi-cians' instructions to patients.

Besides the obvious tasks (the bulleted list), even the "basic job description" which precedes it has clear tasks you can pull out. "Schedule appointments," "maintain records," "take and record vital signs." The mission is for us to mine these documents for tasks. Hopefully clear tasks. Tasks which capture the job's requirements and therefore the training items.

Pulling out the tasks

When you look at any position and the accompanying documentation, you try to pull out the tasks hidden beneath the jargon. You can ask the simple question, "what does the position require you to do?"

When you pull tasks, many times you have to reword them to be effective. You have to ensure they lead with an action verb (I'm talking tasks here), ensure they are actually tasks for *this* job, and you need to avoid compounds. If you have a compound statement for your task, it means there's actually more than one task. Before you can evaluate it – break it down to remove the ambiguity inherent in compounds.

So, your first step is to pull the tasks out of the position descriptions. This technique can be used for all existing documentation; job postings, performance evaluations, process documents, checklists, etc. You mine the documentation for anything which is a task, infers a task, or could indicate a hidden task. You start by looking for verbs. Tasks should always be the performance of X. Yes, you might care about the reason you perform the task…but for your purposes you only care about the why as a means to ensure you haven't missed any hidden tasks.

From the Waiter/Waitress job description:

"Check with customers to ensure that they are enjoying their meals and take action to correct any problems."

If you do a simple literal translation you see that you actually have more than one task:

1. Check with customers

2. Ensure customers are enjoying their meals

3. Correct any problems

From a metrics-foundation, I'd offer that asking the customer is only *one* way you might determine if the customer is enjoying their meal and should *not* be taken as the only way to do so. Many customers won't tell you that they aren't happy with their meal. If the real goal is to ensure they are enjoying their meal, "checking with customers" may not get you the answer. This is another good reason to break the task out – you may find out the priority of tasks – for example you may find that ensuring satisfaction was the most important task. Correcting problems is a means to that particular end as is checking with customers.

So, the task may be rewritten to be "ensure customers enjoy their meals" with subtasks of "check with them" and "correct any problems." But the beauty of capturing the tasks is that you don't have to worry about the order or priority (yet). You just have to capture them all because you very well may need to train the worker on how to do each part.

Notice that each of the tasks identified starts with a verb.

Notice how breaking out the tasks adds clarity to what is expected.

If you were developing the training (which comes much later) you'd appreciate the rewording, but would still need to do a further breakdown. What goes into "Checking with customers?" Do you ask if they want anything? Do you check to see if they have eaten the food? Do you check to see if they are drinking their beverages? Do you look for signs of displeasure? Should they be happy?

What goes into correcting problems? How much power/autonomy does the wait staff have to correct the problems?

A trainer will be very happy to receive a clear list of tasks (broken down to the appropriate levels) and clarity around the level of performance expected. The supporting knowledge and skills necessary to get the trainee to the point of proficiency should be left to the trainer. It's how different schools are formed. If the task is to "defend yourself against an attacker" you might find dozens of schools of thought and training on how to perform that meta-task. Depending on the task breakdown you'll narrow the training down from martial arts, military arts, weapon use, and basic self-defense training. But even then, there are many different ways to teach someone to block a punch, break a choke hold, or avoid being struck.

You have to focus on the task, not the skills and knowledge – those will change much faster than the end task. And that change is a good thing…you may find more effective or efficient ways to perform a task if you are not overly restrictive on the process.

So to say it as simply as possible:

"Start with the task."

Other sources
Besides the position description, there are many possible sources for determining the tasks which go into a job. I mentioned the Job

Posting, Performance Evaluation, and Process Documentation. Here is a more complete list of possible sources; you should be able to find a few new ones as you delve deeper into the effort.

Job posting
Like the position description, this document is normally used when advertising the job. You'll find job postings differ from the position description though because their purposes are seen as different. The position description helps the human resources department determine salary scales and management levels. It also helps with the performance evaluation. Most times the position description is used as a source document for the job posting.

The job posting is a shorter version of the position description used solely to communicate the hiring needs. It's used publicly to advertise the job and solicit interest from potential hires. Even if your organization doesn't use position descriptions, chances are they have created job postings for any open positions. Of course if you are building a development plan for a filled position, you may have to dig a little to find old job postings.

Performance evaluation
Past (and present) performance evaluations can be a good source of tasks for a given position. You're not concerned with how well the person performed the tasks – I strip all of the evaluative information from the document. All you want are the underlying tasks. Performance evaluations can be especially useful because they normally focus on the more critical tasks to be performed. Of course you can't use them in isolation as they won't touch on the majority of tasks performed – there's usually just too much to be done. You also tend to miss the "easier" tasks or the tasks which the worker is expert at because those don't tend to be reflected on annual reviews.

TIP: Filter the List

Look for tasks that are administrative in nature, or are universal non-position tasks (a possible indicator is if a task is performed outside of, or throughout, the process lifecycle). These tasks should be removed from this listing since you are attempting to create a position specific MTL. The data can be saved by the work center to be included in their documentation. All good processes create useful byproducts. This process is especially rich in producing valuable byproducts. I've already stressed the benefits to communications between the worker and supervisor – but all documentation you produce will have some value.

Process documents

Process definitions are a great place to find material for your MTL. If a process is defined, you will have a great source for your tasks. Each step in the process is normally described as a task and if the process definition is well written, you'll even have a viable task breakdown. Remember to look hard at the steps in the process to ensure they are at a low-enough level for use as a task.

If your processes are not defined, check for process definitions from other organizations, the internet, or even your library. Process definitions are one of the rare cases where you can leverage other organization's work. An existing process definition can be used as is (if the stars align perfectly) but most times they will work as a great starting point for your own. There will usually be differences in procedures, rules, and policies…but what you'll have is a great starting point.

Review other existing documentation

Review existing documentation that may help identify tasks by position. This could include; work schedules, workflow diagrams, job postings for other companies, and training offerings. Training offerings can work if you don't stop there. If you find a well-written training offering you'll have a list of tasks they will train to. But don't decide that you now don't have to create a plan because you found the training you need! Until you've built your MTL and then assessed your workers against that list, you can't be sure that the training is needed (for a particular worker), comprehensive, or of good quality.

Survey, Question, or Interview Personnel

The person currently filling the position can be surveyed, questioned, and interviewed to gain information about the job. It's logical that the person who does the job has the best feel for the requirements of that position. It's like asking the quarterback what he does in his role. This can be enlightening even to the best coach. Many times coaches (leaders and managers too) take things for granted and don't notice some of the tasks that go into the position. One simple example is if you ask a player about his responsibilities, chances are you'll hear "communicate with the coach" or "interpret the coach's direction for new players." But if you ask the coach for a list of tasks the player performs, these types of tasks will be omitted from the list. You forget about these types of tasks.

That said, you still want to query the supervisors – this will not only help validate the worker's views but it's a great loop closer. You'll see later that comparing what the worker thinks he is supposed to do and what the supervisor expects him to do is a valuable benefit from creating the development plan.

Now that you've built a draft list of tasks you'll need to polish up it.

Produce Task Breakdowns

The goal of this step is to break tasks down into the lowest level of task necessary. The question that may be haunting you is, "How do I know which level to go down to when doing a task breakdown?" Or, "When have I gone far enough?" Some may be obviously at too high a level, like "supervise" or "manage a project." These require a breakdown to understand how to evaluate them. Here are four pieces of advice that should help:

a. The 101 Test
b. List only the *whats*, not the *hows*
c. If a new person filling the position could identify all the sub-tasks, that is low enough
d. If the performance of a sub-task is intuitive, do not list it (under "conducting a meeting", do not list "attend meeting")

The 101 Test

This is the easiest, and one of the best ways I've found to determine if your task requires a break down. Take the task (verb and object) and add "101" after it. Does it sound like a class you would take? If it does, it needs a task breakdown. For example, if you listed "manage project" as a task, add "101" and you get Managing Projects 101. Yup, sounds like an introductory class you'd take from the Project Management Institute ®. So, break it down:

• Manage project budget
• Manage project scope
• Manage project schedule
• Manage project resources

Any of those could be the next level of task below "manage project." You easily could put 101 after these and still decide you might find it in a course brochure. So, go a little lower:

Manage project budget becomes:

• Estimate costs
• Create spend plan
• Track expenditures against budget
• Make adjustments as necessary

You may come up with other sub tasks – the point is that you can continue the breakdown until you get to tasks that you would expect to see as part of the training, not the title of the course.

Sometimes I find clients who offer up a task that could easily be the title for a college or program, much less a course! Manage projects actually fits this example. I would not be surprised to find an entire program called Project Management in which the first breakdown of budget, scope, schedule, and resources would be specific courses. I can even imagine a College of Project Management. So, use the 101 test if you're not sure a task should be broken down.

List only the whats, not the hows
If you catch yourself capturing how a task is performed (process steps or procedural components), stop. You're going too far. While a step-by-step guide is useful, it is not a necessity. As long as you have the "what" for each task, you can build a plan. But as with all things – don't throw away the information if you catch yourself going too far. You'll want to build process definitions for your more complex efforts and this information will be useful. But, for the professional development plan, this is more than what you need.

If a new person filling the position could identify all the subtasks, that is low enough
In fact, this is a good way to do the task breakdown. The new person in any organization has a valuable viewpoint. The new hire's point of view is not encumbered by the "that's the way we've always done it" syndrome. They see everything in a new, unfiltered light. At least if they have filters, it's a new set of filters affording you a different take on things you may be taking for granted. It never fails to amaze me how much we take for granted.

If you've been doing the same things, the same way, for any appreciable amount of time – chances are you would have a lot of trouble explaining (in detail) what you do. You leave out things that to you are obvious and old hat. But to a new worker or someone who doesn't know your job, the description you provide would be full of knowledge holes. Large chasms of "what comes after X and before Y?"

Using a new hire's perspective is a great way to do a task break-down. If you don't have a new hire, try describing the role (in tasks) to someone from a different department. The less the person knows about the position, the better.

If the performance of a sub-task is intuitive, do not list it
For example, under "conducting a meeting", do not list "attend meet-ing". This is more of a guideline, than a rule. Actually all of these suggestions are guidelines. If in doubt, it's better to break a task down too far than not far enough. The good news is that if you fail to break it down far enough, you'll notice when trying to evaluate the ability of the staff to perform the task. For example, if you were eval-uating a worker's ability to conduct a meeting, you wouldn't need to evaluate if they attended the meeting…this would be an obvious re-quirement. But you'll also determine if you need more than "con-duct." You'll decide easily enough if you need to include "schedule, open, control, and end" the meeting as subtasks.

It's all about communication. Break the tasks down far enough so you can fully communicate the level of performance necessary to do the task.

Find Logical Groupings for Tasks
Many times the tasks in the MTL can be grouped under a larger heading. This step is optional, but recommended. It will make it eas-ier to work with the plan if the list of tasks are organized into logical groupings. This is best accomplished through process definitions. As you are building the MTL you probably did so in relation to re-

sponsibilities or processes. But if you have a laundry list without logical groupings, you can start by asking these questions and aligning the tasks based on your answers.

1. Is there an expected outcome for the task? If so, what other tasks support this same outcome?
2. Are these tasks dependent on each other? Are any prerequisites to others?
3. Check those job descriptions and process definitions; most already have the groupings identified.

Tasks don't exist in a vacuum. If you have a task that is living on its own with no relationship to other tasks your task is either at an extremely high level or you're missing a grouping. So another good test for task breakdowns is if the task doesn't fit with your groupings, it probably will benefit from a breakdown.

While you're identifying groupings, a valuable byproduct will be the mapping you create. When you are looking for courses to satisfy the training needs, the groupings should equate to course titles or at the least, criterion referenced objectives.

You'll likely find that many minor tasks and sub-tasks are repeated in different processes. These commonalities should be documented. If the commonalities occur in multiple areas, it indicates a possible new grouping.

One way to visually communicate the groupings is to show their relationship to the lifecycle phases of their parent process. This can be accomplished through a table, shading in the phases where the tasks are performed.

Let's do a quick recap.

Rules 1 and 2; Each task has to start with a verb and must actually be a job requirement.

Review Existing Documentation to include:

- Job descriptions
- Job postings
- Performance evaluations
- Process documents
- Training offerings

Ask the people doing the job.

Ask the supervisors of those doing the job.

Pull out the tasks:

- Find the Verb and Object in the sentence
- If the wording lacks a clear verb/object, modify to find them

Produce Task Breakdowns:

- Some tasks will be too low of a level – and you'll need to work back up to a reasonable task definition
- Most will be too high of a level, requiring you to break the task down.
- Very few will be at the proper level
    - The 101 Test
    - List only the whats, not the hows
    - If a new person filling the position could identify all the sub-tasks, that is low enough
    - If the performance of a sub-task is intuitive, do not list it (under "conducting a meeting", do not list "attend meeting")

Find logical groupings for the tasks

- Is there an expected outcome for the task? If so, what other tasks support this same outcome?
- Are these tasks dependent on each other? Are any prerequisites to others?
- Check those job descriptions and process definitions; most already have the groupings identified.

Chapter 3-2
Define Training Requirements

Task attributes

There are four attributes used to describe each task:

1. Frequency to Perform – how often the task is performed
2. Complexity to Perform – how difficult the task is to carry out
3. Complexity to Learn/Teach – how hard it is to learn
4. Criticality – how important is it to get the task right the first time

For each of the tasks you will set a value for each attribute. These values are relative and subjective. Each attribute is rated High (H), Medium (M) or Low (L). Based on this subjective rating, you can determine important information for creation of a professional development plan:

1. If the task requires training.
2. If the training should be supplemented with a checklist, quality check, job aid or thorough instructions.
3. What type of training will work best; On-the-Job, Just-in-Time, self-paced, computer-based, or formal training.

You can use a table to list every task and capture your ratings.

Task	Frequency	Complexity to Perform	Complexity to Learn	Criticality
Task 1				
Sub Task 1a				
Sub Task 1b				
Task 2				

Figure 4, sample table

I will offer one set of possible values for your ratings; an example of a range you can use. In the end, you have to determine the right breakpoints for each factor based on your situation and culture.

Frequency
Give each task a rating for how frequently the task is performed.

> High (H) = if you do the task daily
> Medium (M) = if you do the task weekly
> Low (L) = if you do the task less frequently than weekly

For each of the tasks, both the worker and supervisor should rate each attribute. You can also survey others – but for most development plans I have found this will be enough. If you feel you want more inputs you can ask co-workers and customers to provide their take on the attributes. Whatever number of people you want to poll, you'll need to ensure they are using the same scale.

Complexity to perform
Let's follow up the easy one (frequency) with a little tougher attribute. Now you'll rate the complexity of the task. Not how "hard" the task is, but how complex or "complicated" it is to perform. For example, finding a needle in the proverbial haystack is extremely hard to

accomplish, but it's not complex. Creating a smartphone app though may be complicated from the beginning. Depending on the type of application the level of complexity may grow exponentially.

> H = Extreme complexity – lots of complicated steps, together creating a complicated process
> M = complex – not as tough as high, but not simple either
> L = Rather simple

As with all of the attributes, both the supervisor and worker should take their best shot at evaluating them. Don't stress out – you can always adjust your ratings later. The first step is to open communications between the supervisor and the worker. I know I told you that open communication was a byproduct of the process, but it may be more accurate to think of the ratings as a byproduct.

Complexity to learn

This may be the most obscure of the evaluation criteria. How complex is it to learn the task? Can you follow simple instructions or must you make decisions throughout the process? If it's easier for you, think about how complex it is to *teach*.

> H = Requires background information, a lot of time and effort
> M = Requires some info, and a decent amount of time/effort
> L = Easy to learn, can teach yourself, little time/effort

The complexity to perform the task and the complexity to learn the task can be thought of as a pair. They work together to determine if the task requires training. It's rare that you'll find one of the pair to be high and the other low.

The last attribute is much easier to determine.

Criticality

Criticality shows how important it is for the task to be done right the first time. Like frequency, this too is subjective and you can use a different scale, but I find that the following works in most cases.

> H = if the task must be done right the first time
> M = if you can take 2-3 times to get it right
> L = if you can take more than 3 tries to get it right

Like all of the attributes, the evaluation of criticality is very subjective. Actually, criticality is even more subjective than the others. The criticality for this task can depend on the situation or the customer. Imagine your task is to restore the customer's email account. If the customer is a coworker, the criticality may be low or at most medium. If the customer is the CEO, the criticality becomes extremely high. Because of this, I usually recommend you use the highest possible rating for each task, with a logical dose of reality. If the task is performed regularly and almost always for a mid-level customer; go with the rating for that majority. You'll deal with the rare case of the CEO being the customer when it occurs. But if the VIP customer is an occasional occurrence, than go with the highest possible rating.

Determining results

Based on the ratings given to each task, it will be classified as a training requirement or not. The ratings will also assist in determining a recommended method of delivery for training and what tools or instruments would improve the processes involved. Rather than show all 81 permutations possible, you can look at two key pairings for your analysis. The two pairings that are used in the analysis are;

1. Complexity to Perform and Complexity to Learn
2. Frequency and Criticality.

The first analysis is to determine if the task requires training. If it doesn't, than you won't need to look at the other pairing.

Training is required if:

 a. Either "Complexity of Task" or "Complexity to Learn" is high
    or
 b. Both "Complexity of Task" and "Complexity to Learn" are me-
    dium

Task	Complexity to Perform	Complexity to Learn	Training Required?	OJT?	Self-Paced Training?	Formal or Knowledge Item?
Task 1	L	L				
Task 1a	L	M				
Task 1b	L	H	Y			Y
Task 2	M	L				
Task 3	M	M	Y			
Task 4	M	H	Y			Y
Task 5	H	L	Y	Y	Y	
Task 6	H	M	Y			Y
Task 7	H	H	Y			Y

Figure 5, determining training requirements

Litmus Test
If the task is not a training requirement, based on the values you gave it for the complexity pair, *and* you are confident that the task will require training, adjust your scores so it comes out as a training requirement. Then use this as a benchmark for the other tasks.

The other major question this analysis will answer is if the task will benefit from formal classroom training or if there's likely a required knowledge component. The answer is "Yes" if Complexity of Task or Complexity to Learn is high.

The second pairing to analyze is Frequency and Criticality. If the task is a training requirement, frequency will dictate the type of training and if tools will be useful.

Task	Frequency	Criticality	Job Aid?	Thorough Instructions?	Checklist?	Quality Check?	JITT
Task 1	L		Y	Y			Y
Task 3		M	Y		Y		
Task 4		H	Y		Y	Y	

Figure 6, frequency and criticality

Tasks will benefit from job aids, thorough instructions, checklists and quality checks in the performance of the job, so feel free to use these recommendations even for tasks which are not training requirements.

The logic follows:

1. If complexity to perform or complexity to learn is high, it is a training requirement.
2. If both complexity to perform and complexity to learn are medium, it is a training requirement.
3. If complexity to perform or complexity to learn is high, the task is also a knowledge requirement. This suggests that training on this task will benefit from "book" knowledge. Usually theories or concepts need to be taught to ensure a full grasp of how to perform the task
4. If criticality is medium or high, a checklist is recommended
5. If criticality is high, a quality check is called for.
6. If frequency is low and it is a training requirement, thorough instructions will help.

7. If complexity to learn/teach is low and it is a training requirement, On-the-Job training is a good fit.
8. If complexity to learn/teach is medium or high and it is a training requirement, formal training is suggested.

Frequency	Complexity of Task	Complexity to Learn	Criticality	Training Requirements	Knowledge Item?	Checklist?	Quality Check?	OJT?	Thorough Instructions?	Formal Training?	JITT	Job Aids
	L	L		N								
	M	L		N								
	L	M		N								
	M	M		Y						Y		
	H			Y	Y							
		H		Y	Y					Y		
			M			Y						
			H			Y	Y					
	H		L					Y				
L				if Y					Y		Y	
L			M									Y
L			H									Y

Figure 7, Attribute Analysis

Chapter 3-3
Determine required skill levels

You analyzed each task using four attributes and the results tell us which tasks require training, recommendations on the delivery methods for those tasks, and which tools or instruments would be helpful in performing the task. It is important to remind you that the previous step, as well as this one, has to be done collaboratively with the worker and supervisor. Throughout the development of the plan, one of the most valuable benefits is this cause of communication.

The next step provides more valuable information. You will determine the level of skill required for the position. If you have multiple positions, say an entry level position, a skilled position, and a lead for the same job, you will have a positional development plan for each.

To assess the required skill level for a position, both the supervisor and worker will independently rate each training requirement on a scale from 1 to 5. There is no need to rate tasks that do not require training. The values are novice, beginner, skilled, supervisor, and expert. (See chapter 2-3 for a breakdown).

You can use a different scale. The idea is to have a system which allows both the worker and the supervisor to evaluate the tasks with enough variation to ensure clarity of rating. To allow more variation I encourage users to score the tasks from 1 to 5 but include decimal values. This allows for a wide range of values while still keeping the key milestones to a smaller range.

Tasks	Worker Score	Supervisor Score	Final Score
Task 1	3	3	3
Task 1a	3	4	4
Task 1b	4	3	3.5
Task 2	2	3.5	3
Task 3	2.75	3.25	3.5
Task 3a	3	4	4
Task 3b	3.5	3	3

Figure 8, sample scores

Once you have scored the tasks separately, combine the results into one table so you can easily see the scores side-by-side as in Figure 8. Each task warrants a short conversation. If the scores are the same then the conversation will be very short. The further apart the scores, the bigger the conversation.

"I thought the task was a three – you should be able to perform it without supervision."

"I was thinking that this role would be our expert on this task and would have to be able to lead others during the process."

"That's actually John's role. This role is more of a support position than the lead; at least for this task."

If you can't come to agreement in 2-3 minutes, take the higher of the two scores and move on. If the higher score is wrong, the only repercussion is the worker may end up getting training she doesn't *need*. My friend Don calls this "erring on the side of excellence."

Notice in the Figure 8 example, the final SCORE is not always the higher of the two choices. During the conversation, the worker and supervisor may agree that the score should be lower, higher or something in between. The rule of erring on the side of excellence is only used when agreement can't be reached easily. And easily means within 3 minutes of discussion. Remember, you can have a different skill-level requirement for different positions, even though they are performing the same task.

Key point

Notice that there are no 1's or 5's on the score sheet. This is because it is unlikely that you will ever require a position to be a novice (it's likely not a training requirement for that position) and almost as rare that you will require an expert.

At this point you have accomplished a lot. You now have a positional professional development plan. Celebrate a little, but not for too long, you want to get right to the next step while everything is fresh in your mind.

Chapter 3-4
Evaluate existing abilities

I prefer that this step be performed immediately after completing the previous step of evaluating the level of skill required for a position. The sooner you get to this step the better. Better because the decisions and discussions you had to produce the required skill ratings will be fresher in your mind.

You will follow the same basic process for identifying the skills of each person filling the position as you did for determining the needs of the position. You are moving from a *positional professional development plan* to a *personal development plan*.

I like the technique of having each person grading the tasks to do so independently at first. Feel free to pull in feedback from others. You can leverage the opinions of coworkers, previous supervisors, and even customers; depending on your relationships with each. If you realize that this may be contentious and want ideas about how to deal with the possible and likely resistance, read the corresponding concept chapter.

When you assign this work to your employee, take a little time up front to discuss the scale you'll be using. I recommend a five point scale with decimal values to provide wider differentiation. Whatever scale you used for the requirement scoring you should also use for the personal evaluations. If you pull in any new evaluators spend a little time reviewing the work you already accomplished.

Rate the worker's ability to perform each training requirement task; what is the worker's skill level? Don't pull any punches. Don't embellish. Don't detract. Be honest with the worker and encourage the worker to be honest with himself.

Remember, use the same values as you used for the requirements:

1. Novice – If the worker is at the Novice level, he can barely perform the task and needs supervision and guidance. He can't perform the task without thorough instructions.
2. Beginner – A worker at the beginner level needs only limited supervision to perform the task. The worker wouldn't have to know when they were getting the wrong results.
3. Skilled – A Skilled worker performs at an "unmanaged" level. The worker can perform the task without guidance or supervision. At the skilled level he knows when he is getting the wrong results, but doesn't know how to adjust to get the right results. This is the most frequently required state.
4. Supervisor – A worker at the Supervisor level performs well enough to train others. A worker at this level can supervise a Beginner or Novice, providing guidance as needed. This worker understands how to resolve issues and troubleshoot problems.
5. Expert – The best you can be. The Expert has mastered the task and can train others. He can evaluate the performance of all levels.

In evaluating the current skills of the worker, all values are fair game. It's common to find worker's skills spanning the entire spectrum, unlike the expectations we have for the requirements (no novice and the rare expert).

Again the key for success is taking advantage of the opportunity for the supervisor and worker to team together. You have another opportunity to excel – you can bring together workers filling the same or similar roles for a group discussion. It will make evaluations easier and more accurate if you can bring together your unit to determine and/or review the ratings together. This is not a reflection of dedication, effort, or potential. The goal is to determine an accurate assessment of where the worker's skill levels lie.

Sound good?

Remember though, while you have the best of intentions, the worker may not hear it the same thing you think you're saying it. Be careful. Be considerate.

This time when you review the scores together you will err on the side of excellence by picking the lower of the two scores if you can't come to an agreement in 3 minutes or less. The consequence if you're wrong is that the worker will end up getting training she didn't really need.

Tasks	Worker Score	Supervisor Score	Final Score
Task 1	3	3	3
Task 1a	3	4	3
Task 1b	4	3	3.5
Task 2	2	3.5	2
Task 3	2.75	3.25	2.5
Task 3a	3	4	3
Task 3b	3.5	4	3

Figure 9, sample scores

This should look familiar because it's the same as you produced for the requirement level, except for choosing the lower score when the choice isn't clear.

Note: I usually find that the worker downplays his own abilities rather than over estimating them.

Now that you have scores for what's required of the worker, take the final scores and put them together.

Tasks	Required Skill Level	Worker's Current Ability
Task 1	3	3
Task 1a	4	3
Task 1b	3.5	3.5
Task 2	3	2
Task 3	3.5	2.5
Task 3a	4	3
Task 3b	3	3.5

Figure 10, sample scores

When you put everything together, you have the basis for a personal professional development plan. Now you need to find out where training is required and make a plan to fill the gaps.

Chapter 3-5
Managing the Gap

Identify the gaps in ability

This step is very easy. No worries, just simple math. Subtract the *worker skill ability* from the *required level*.

Tasks	Required Skill Level	Worker's Current Ability	Gap
Task 1	3	3	0
Task 1a	4	3	-1
Task 1b	3.5	3.5	0
Task 2	3	2	-1
Task 3	3.5	2.5	-1
Task 3a	4	3	-1
Task 3b	3	3.5	.5

Figure 11, sample scores

Wherever you have a negative gap, you have an opportunity for improvement; a need for training. Wherever you have a positive gap, the worker has a higher skill than required.

Prioritizing the gaps

In the spirit of providing a practical step-by-step process, I'll tell you up front; I consider this step to be optional. Although, it will be useful, especially when you have choices between tasks to train, it's in no way mandatory. You do not have to adhere to the priorities you set. The idea is that it may be useful, but it's not required.

That said, if you find that you like the idea of knowing which tasks should be trained first, carry on.

Once you've identified the gaps, you can work to prioritize which gaps you want to fill first. There are many considerations, including availability of training, groupings, and the need. The step is pretty simple...after determining your prioritization, document it using numbers or letters to signify the results. This is a tool for helping in the scheduling of training. It is not restrictive. If you find an offering that works for you, use it, regardless of the priority. But, if you have a choice, the prioritization can help you choose.

Tasks	Required Skill Level	Worker's Current Ability	Gap	Prioritization
Task 1	3	3	0	
Task 1a	4	3	-1	c
Task 1b	3.5	3.5	0	
Task 2	3	2	-1	d
Task 3	3.5	2.5	-1	a
Task 3a	4	3	-1	b
Task 3b	3	3.5	.5	

Figure 12, sample scores

You won't need to set a priority for tasks which don't have a negative gap since they don't require training. As promised; simple and short.

Chapter 3-6
Selecting Training Vehicles

This step is primarily a concept question, rather than a practicum issue. The best advice is to find training which delivers measurable value for your training dollars. This means that the vendor is less on the hook than you are. You have to evaluate the effectiveness of the training so that you can make intelligent decisions.

Identify the type of training

Go back to our four attributes and the resulting recommendations. What is the type of training recommended? Most of the selection process will be concerned with finding formal training but any training you pay for will benefit from you focusing on choosing the proper vendor. It's not enough to check the marketing materials for the training. You should find peers or comparable organizations who have used the vendor. The catch though is that most organizations and individuals lack a comprehensive professional development plan, so chances are no one will have evaluated the offerings against a well-defined set of tasks!

You most likely will be the first.

If you find yourself in this situation (and I'm betting you most likely will), you can still do better than throwing a dart at the wall. Since you have your tasks broken down, you've evaluated them against the four attributes, and you have assessed the level of skill you need to attain, you can compare what you want to learn against what the vendor claims to deliver. Ask for the training's criterion referenced objectives. Ask what tasks are covered and to what level of skill.

Don't be surprised if the vendor gives you a blank stare. Since most customers simply throw money at the vendor and hope for the best, you'll likely encounter confusion and ignorance. Chances are, even if the vendor has the answers to your very logical questions, the sales person with whom you are working with does not. Don't be surprised if they have to put you in contact with the instructor.

So don't settle.

Don't ask them if they will do what you want; they'll happily claim the training will suffice. Instead ask them what their training will cover, what tasks it includes, and what level of skill can you expect to walk out the door with for your investment.

Chapter 3-7
Scheduling, assessing, and tracking training

In the concept section of this book I said that this should be a single line on a to-do list. In other words, this will be a very short chapter.

Scheduling

Once you've selected the training method (OJT, In-house, On-site, Formal, On-line, Computer-based, or Self-paced training), you'll want to select a source. I'd put the highest weight on quality of training; before cost and availability. But I'm a purist. Once you've selected the method and the source, you'll review the offerings so you can schedule the training.

Make this appointment untouchable. There's no faster way to tell your organization that the staff doesn't really matter than to make their development a low priority. And there's no better way to convey that they are unimportant than to usurp a scheduled training session for the latest crisis in the organization.

You may not think twice about calling in an important member of the team off vacation to fix a critical issue. Of course you'd be wrong for your callousness, but hey I'm not trying to tell you how to be a good leader. When it comes to training though – do more than think twice. Or better yet, don't think about it at all...just don't do it. Schedule it and keep to that schedule. Work around the problem. You'd not try to get that worker back if he were undergoing surgery, were on his honeymoon, or was meeting with the president of the company...don't do it if he is attending scheduled training.

This is a great opportunity to prove how important the job is, how important the worker is, and how important the worker's skills are to the success of the organization. Don't blow it by conveying that the development of that worker's skills are secondary to whatever the latest crisis is.

So, schedule it in your preferred tool. Mark the worker as Out-of-Office. And then don't allow your worker to break that appointment.

I told you it would be short.

Assessing training

In the concept section I covered the reasons you assess the training. Here I will give a few examples of how the assessment may go. First we will use the development plan template to reassess the skill level of the trainee. Realize though that you may not see an improvement right away. So, consider this a first look. Ask the worker some simple questions, and of course *listen* to the answers.

1. Was the training worth the cost?
2. What did you like about the training?
3. What didn't you like?
4. What tasks do you feel that you can perform better?
5. Should we send others to this training or should we try a different source?
6. How much of what you learned do you feel comfortable sharing with others?
7. What would you rate your skill now on the tasks covered?
8. When do you think we should reassess your skill levels for these tasks?

Use the plan to document the answers – especially the ones concerning new skill levels.

Track progress against the plan

As you have the conversations with your worker make sure that you track her progress in the plan. Do it together. The plan is shared property. It's important to have a visual, tangible tool for the manager and worker to look at when discussing progress. It helps in all plans and the development plan is no exception. You can use an application to track progress. You can track it on paper. The medium is not the message. The key is for you to actively track it.

The medium is not the message.

Audit

This step is easy – if it's being done through a software application, check for last date modified. See how often it has been updated. If you are using paper and pencil, check to see how often it is used. Is there dust on the spine? This step should be regularly reviewed. The best way to see if professional development is alive and well in your organization is to audit your development plans. If you don't have professional development plans for each position, chances are you aren't actively developing your personnel.

Chapter 3-8
A Sport Walkthrough

I love using unrelated professions to teach skills. For my High School varsity girls' volleyball team, I brought in a football coach to teach the girls how to properly throw a football. It was a great practice. I passed out mini-footballs, one for every two girls and we went through drills Pop Warner youth were doing. After an hour the girls weren't throwing like "girls" any longer and they enjoyed their new skill. Then I showed them how the exact same motion they used to throw the football was how they should be hitting the volleyball. We spend the rest of the practice hitting. For the rest of the season, whenever I felt their technique getting sloppy, we went back to throwing the football. This also works with throwing a softball or baseball from the outfield. The same motion. I call it cross-training. It keeps practices fun and challenging.

I offered this aside for two reasons. The first is that I'm going to borrow a training technique from video games. My son grew up in the age of Halo ® and Elder Scrolls ®. In each case a favorite gift on his wish list was a walkthrough. Sometimes these are found free online and sometimes you have to purchase them. A walkthrough takes you step by step through the video game, telling you where all the special items are and how to navigate the tricks and traps. I'm going to borrow this concept and provide you with a walkthrough of the process.

The second reason I used a volleyball story as the introduction is that the example I will use is for the position of Outside (Ace) hitter for a volleyball team. Being the practicum section, feel free to skim through as much of the detail as you like. I provide it for comprehensiveness – but I don't expect you to read it all.

Master Task Listing – Volleyball Team (Sport)

As mentioned in the concept section, you can develop an MTL for an entire unit or area within your organization. I first created an MTL for the entire volleyball team. This was especially useful for me since I wanted all of my players to have a good understanding of the skills involved for every position. Volleyball, like most sports and jobs has become very specialized. But, in all cases, there is a clear benefit in cross-training and expanding the breadth of skill and knowledge of the entire team.

The basic tasks are:

1. Hitting
2. Setting
3. Passing
4. Serving
5. Blocking

Using the 101 test, each of these could easily be the title of a separate course. The first level of breakdown was also easy.

1. Hitting
    a. Left Side
    b. Middle
    c. Right Side
    d. Backrow
    e. Playsets
2. Setting
    a. Left Side
    b. Middle
    c. Right Side
    d. Backrow
    e. Playsets
3. Passing
    a. Serve Receive
    b. Digging
4. Serving

  a. Jump serve
  b. Topspin
  c. Float
  d. Side spin
 5. Blocking
  a. Setting the block
  b. Joining the block
  c. Blocking solo

Within each of these subsets, there are variants or techniques to consider. The final list I came up with follows:

Hitting
 Hit an outside set on Left side
  Hit a Shoot
  Hit a high outside set (left side)
  Hit a mid-range, loop (left side)
  Hit a mid-range shoot (left side)
 Hit a middle set
  Hit a middle quick-set
  Hit a middle "high" set
  Hit a middle back quick
  Hit a middle back "high" set
 Hit a right side set
  Hit a high outside set (right side)
  Hit a mid-range loop (right side)
  Hit a mid-range shoot (right side)
  Hit a slide (right side)
 Hit a Playset
  Be the first hitter in a playset
   Hit a Tandem playset (first hitter)
   Hit an X playset (first hitter)
   Hit a cross play set (first hitter)
   Hit a Stack playset (first hitter)
  Playset second hitter
   Hit a Tandem playset (second hitter)
   Hit an X playset (second hitter)
   Hit a Cross playset (second hitter)

Hit a Stack playset (second hitter)
Hit a backrow attack
Hit a backrow attack (Left)
Hit a backrow attack (Pipe)
Hit a backrow attack (Right)
Player control shots
Hit a cut shot
Hit a dink/dump
Hit a roll shot
Tool the block
Hit a power wipe
Hit off block for second chance

Setting

Set an outside set on Left side
Set a Shoot (left side)
Set a high outside (left side)
Set a mid-range, loop (left side)
Set a mid-range shoot (left side)
Set a middle set
Set a middle quick-set
Set a middle "high" set
Set a middle back quick
Set a middle back "high" set
Set a right side set
Set a high outside set (right side)
Set a mid-range loop (right side)
Set a mid-range shoot (right side)
Set a Slide (right side)
Set a Playset
Set a Tandem playset
Set an X playset
Set a Cross playset
Set a Stack playset
Set a Backrow attack
Set a backrow attack (Left)
Set backrow attack (Pipe)
Set a backrow attack (Right)
Player control sets
One hand sets

Pulling sets out of net
Bringing sets back from over

Passing
Serve Receive
Serve Receive Underhand
Serve Receive Jump serve (underhand)
Serve Receive Top Spin (underhand)
Serve Receive Float (underhand)
Serve Receive side spin (underhand)
Serve Receive up tempo (underhand)
Overhand Serve Receive
Serve Receive Jump serve (overhand)
Serve Receive Top spin (overhand)
Serve Receive Float (overhand)
Serve Receive side spin (overhand)
Serve Receive up tempo (overhand)
Digging
Digging power side hit
Digging right side hit
Digging middle hits
Digging off speed hits
Digging dinks/dumps
Digging roll shots
Digging deflections off blocks
Digging blocked balls
Digging emergency passes
Digging dive
Digging roll
Digging one arm

Serving
Serve a jump serve
Serve a top spin serve
Serve a float serve
Serve a side spin serve

Blocking
Solo Block
Solo Block - Left

Solo Block - Right
Solo Block – Middle
Set the Block
Set Block - Left
Set Block – Right
Join the Block
Middle Block
Soft Block

As you can see, the list of tasks can become long, especially if you are attempting to be comprehensive. The good news is that the effort is well worth it. You will have a complete task list and therefore a complete understanding of what goes into the unit's performance as well as what goes into a given position. At the beginning of each year, I pass out an MTL for each position with prose which explains what those tasks entail. I also include the attitude needed to play the position.

I have also done the analysis of the four factors for each task. The Left or Ace Hitter is usually a key passer on the team. This is not mandatory though. It happens most times because the left side hitter is usually your best overall athlete. As such she usually ends up being one of your better passers. But, for the purpose of this book I'm only going to include the hitting set of skills; the hitter could in theory be subbed out of the back row. The left side hitter has to also be a blocker. She also may have to set if there is an out-of-system play. And depending on your team, she also may need to serve. I'm leaving all of these out of this portion to simplify your reading. .

Master Task Listing – Attribute Assessment (Sport)

This assessment reflects my personal view of the four factors. A different coach or player may have a different opinion.

Task	Frequency	Complexity of Task	Complexity to Learn	Criticality
Hit on Left side	H	H	H	M
Hit a Shoot	L	H	H	H
Hit a high outside set	H	M	M	L
Hit a mid-range, loop	M	H	H	M
Hit a mid-range shoot	L	H	H	H
Playset second hitter	M	H	H	H
Hit a Tandem playset	M	H	H	H
Hit an X playset	L	H	H	H
Hit a Cross playset	L	H	H	H
Hit a Stack playset	M	H	H	H
Hit a cut shot	M	H	H	H
Hit a dink/dump	M	M	M	M
Hit a roll shot	L	M	M	M
Tool the block	M	H	H	H
Hit a power wipe	M	M	M	M
Hit off block for second chance	L	H	H	H

Figure 13, four attributes

Based on this analysis we have the following results

Task	Frequency	Complexity of Task	Complexity to Learn	Criticality	Training Requirements	Knowledge Item?	Checklist?	Quality Check?	OJT?	Thorough Instructions?	Formal Training?	JITT	Job Aids
Hit on Left side	H	H	H	M	Y	Y	Y	N	N	N	Y	N	N
Hit a Shoot	L	H	H	H	Y	Y	Y	Y	N	Y	Y	Y	Y
Hit a high outside set	H	M	M	L	Y	N	N	N	N	N	Y	N	N
Hit a mid-range, loop	M	H	H	M	Y	Y	Y	N	N	N	Y	N	N
Hit a mid-range shoot	L	H	H	H	Y	Y	Y	Y	N	Y	Y	Y	Y
Playset second hitter	M	H	H	H	Y	Y	Y	Y	N	N	Y	N	N
Hit a Tandem playset	M	H	H	H	Y	Y	Y	Y	N	N	Y	N	N
Hit an X playset	L	H	H	H	Y	Y	Y	Y	N	Y	Y	Y	Y
Hit a Cross playset	L	H	H	H	Y	Y	Y	Y	N	Y	Y	Y	Y
Hit a Stack playset	M	H	H	H	Y	Y	Y	Y	N	N	Y	N	N
Hit a cut shot	M	H	H	H	Y	Y	Y	Y	N	N	Y	N	N
Hit a dink/dump	M	M	M	M	Y	N	Y	N	N	N	Y	N	N
Hit a roll shot	L	M	M	M	Y	N	Y	N	N	Y	Y	N	Y
Tool the block	M	H	H	H	Y	Y	Y	Y	N	N	Y	N	N
Hit a power wipe	M	M	M	M	Y	N	Y	N	N	N	Y	N	N
Hit off block for second chance	L	H	H	H	Y	Y	Y	Y	N	Y	Y	Y	Y

Figure 14, attribute analysis

Master Task Listing – skill level assessment (sport)

The next step is to assess the required skill levels for each task. There is no specific timing for developing any of the job aids or training tools suggested. The hitters will receive extensive practical training. They will also be provided with as much extra information as possible – training videos and videos of themselves performing the tasks. They will also receive quality checks in the form of coaching during practice, matches, and during video review.

In this example, I've aggregated the player's assessments of the required skill levels. We normally have two starting players for each position and one backup. Larger teams may have a second backup, but on the teams I've coached we only carry 12 players as a maximum.

Task	Frequency	Complexity of Task	Complexity to Learn	Criticality	Training Requirements	Required Skill (coach)	Required Skill (Player)	Final Score
Hit on Left side	H	H	H	M	Y	4	4	4
Hit a Shoot	L	H	H	H	Y	3	4	4
Hit a high outside set	H	M	M	L	Y	4	4	4
Hit a mid-range, loop	M	H	H	M	Y	3	4	4
Hit a mid-range shoot	L	H	H	H	Y	3	4	4
Playset second hitter	M	H	H	H	Y	3.5	3	3.5
Hit a Tandem playset	M	H	H	H	Y	4	3	4
Hit an X playset	L	H	H	H	Y	2	3	3
Hit a Cross playset	L	H	H	H	Y	2	3	3
Hit a Stack playset	M	H	H	H	Y	4	3	4
Hit a cut shot	M	H	H	H	Y	4	3	4
Hit a dink/dump	M	M	M	M	Y	4	3	4
Hit a roll shot	L	M	M	M	Y	3	3	3
Tool the block	M	H	H	H	Y	4	3	4
Hit a power wipe	M	M	M	M	Y	3.5	3	3.5
Hit off block for second chance	L	H	H	H	Y	3.5	3	3.5

Figure 15, required assessment

After determining the required skill, we determine where the player currently is.

Task	Frequency	Complexity of Task	Complexity to Learn	Criticality	Training Requirements	Required Skill (Agreed)	Current Skill (Coach)	Current Skill (Worker)	Final Score
Hit on Left side	H	H	H	M	Y	4	3.25	3.25	3.25
Hit a Shoot	L	H	H	H	Y	4	2	2	2
Hit a high outside set	H	M	M	L	Y	4	3	3	3
Hit a mid-range, loop	M	H	H	M	Y	4	2.5	2.5	2.5
Hit a mid-range shoot	L	H	H	H	Y	4	2	2	2
Playset second hitter	M	H	H	H	Y	3.5	1	1	1
Hit a Tandem playset	M	H	H	H	Y	4	1	1	1
Hit an X playset	L	H	H	H	Y	3	1	1	1
Hit a Cross playset	L	H	H	H	Y	3	1	1	1
Hit a Stack playset	M	H	H	H	Y	4	1	1	1
Hit a cut shot	M	H	H	H	Y	4	1	1	1
Hit a dink/dump	M	M	M	M	Y	4	2	2	2
Hit a roll shot	L	M	M	M	Y	3	3	3	3
Tool the block	M	H	H	H	Y	4	1	1	1
Hit a power wipe	M	M	M	M	Y	3.5	1	1	1
Hit off block for second chance	L	H	H	H	Y	3.5	1	1	1

Figure 16, skill assessment

With three players filling this position, the next step is to evaluate each player. In this scenario, this evaluation is extra helpful as it can be used to help determine the first string (the two starters) and among those two who the lead will be. In volleyball lineups, many times your A1, best left-side hitter, starts in the left front, position 4, to allow her to be at the net the maximum amount of time. As in any job selection process – there are other factors that should determine who gets the job. Attitude, chemistry with the rest of the team, and how players perform under pressure. All of these matter, sometimes more than skill levels. But, the information provided by a development plan helps greatly.

Wherever there is a gap in skill, I documented when I'd train the players on the deficiencies. Sometimes a player failed to achieve the desired level during the season. And that's ok. The idea is that the player and the coach both clearly know what the players' strengths and weaknesses are – in relation to the tasks required to perform at a competitive level. Besides practices, the players could obtain outside help from specialists. If this development plan was for a school team, the player may ask her club coach to work with her on the deficiencies during the club season.

The same will happen with workers. Besides the formal training and On-The-Job training, the worker may seek out coaching on her own.

I know as a coach and as a parent I greatly appreciated the open communications the development plan provided. I could have an intelligent conversation, devoid of emotional baggage, about each players' abilities and skills. Essential to our team's success was to ensure that every player understood that our goal wasn't simply to win. Our main goal was to become as good a team and as good individually as we could. The identification of weaknesses and strengths wasn't used to demote or promote a player ahead of another. It was used to help each player reach her potential. This has to be true in the work place also.

Here is a sample of the development priorities for the third string left-side hitter.

Task	Required Skill (Agreed)	Current Skill (Agreed)	% Trained	Priority
Hit on Left side	4	3.25	81%	A
Hit a Shoot	4	2	50%	C
Hit a high outside set	4	3	75%	A
Hit a mid-range, loop	4	2.5	63%	B
Hit a mid-range shoot	4	2	50%	B
Playset second hitter	3.5	1	29%	C
Hit a Tandem playset	4	1	25%	C
Hit an X playset	3	1	33%	D
Hit a Cross playset	3	1	33%	D
Hit a Stack playset	4	1	25%	C
Hit a cut shot	4	1	25%	B
Hit a dink/dump	4	2	50%	A
Hit a roll shot	3	3	100%	C
Tool the block	4	1	25%	A
Hit a power wipe	3.5	1	29%	B
Hit off block for second chance	3.5	1	29%	C

Figure 17, gap analysis with priority

Note: The percentage trained is calculated by dividing the current skill by the required skill level.

As you can see, this player had deficiencies in all the required skills. And this is in part why she was the third string player. The other two players in the position were more skilled than she was, although they may have been at an equal or lower level on a specific skill. This player was also a beginner in volleyball. If I were only selecting team players based on their current skill set, she wouldn't have made the team. But, she had a great attitude, was a hard worker, and had enough athleticism to convince me she had great potential.

Based on personality factors, physical attributes, and her work ethic I chose to groom her for the left-side hitter position. We were able to track her progress and see her grow throughout the season.

Master Task Listing – Schedule (Sport)

You can track the planned training any way you like – I tend to use spreadsheets because I'm familiar with them. The essential things to track are:

1. The task (easy one huh?)
2. The required skill level (so you can monitor improvement)
3. The skill level before training. This will hopefully change after each training session.
4. Priority. This is optional, but I find it helpful to clearly communicate with the trainee which tasks you feel are more important. In the case of the third string player, for her to get more time on the court I needed her to be more effective at high outside sets and loop sets. We were running a "quick" system so she also needed to get the shoot down pat quickly. The playsets were not critical and were of a lower priority. I also needed to help her pick at least two control shots to make a higher priority to give her variety in her attacks.
5. Training Start Date - planned and actual. This is important for showing my commitment as her coach and to make it clear that I expected her to work on these skills.
6. Training – what did we try? Did I use cross training and teach her to throw a football? Did she work with a personal coach? What drills helped her and which didn't work? I needed to document these in the results.
7. Results – skill level after training. This helps for evaluating the effectiveness of the training provided. This gives us insight into which types of training worked and which didn't. Granted each player is different; so what works for one may

not work for another…but I'd prefer trying something that worked for one first, and avoid the training that didn't seem to help.

Here is an example of how you could track the training.

Training	Date Plan	Date Done	Source	Tasks	Skill level pre-trng	Required	Skill level post trng	% trained
Team Practice - Hitting Drills 1 - 3	2/1/2014	2/1/2014	Team Practice	Hit a dink/dump	3	4		75%
Private Coaching - John Spelling	3/5/2014	4/7/2014	Krush Volleyball Training Network	Tool the block	3	4		75%
Football Throw - Bill Reagan	4/7/2014	4/7/2014	Local Football Coach	Hit a high outside set	3	4		75%
Private Coaching - Assistant Coach Jill	4/8/2014	4/8/2014	Assistant Coach	Hit a mid-range, loop	2.5	4		63%

Figure 18, tracking training

You can include any information you like. I usually include the priority for each, and this priority was used for ordering these training items.

Let's try another one.

Chapter 3-9
A Business Position Walkthrough

Adult Service Assistant – Public Library

As fortune has it, I was working with our local library to create professional development plans for the Executive Director and her staff. As I was facilitating the process, I realized that this position plan would make a great example for the book. I set about following the process outlined in this book.

First we gathered existing documentation which included a job description and a later modification to the job definition communicated in a letter from the Executive Director. The position wasn't new, but the director had created a specialty within the department to focus on event planning and programming.

I worked with the person filling the role and her immediate supervisor, the Adult Services Department Manager. As I've mentioned many times – this conversation was the main goal of our effort. It was a good beginning.

Note: While there were five people filling this position, the plan I share with you here was for that specialist.

Master Task Listing – Position (Business)

The basic tasks for an Adult Service Assistant at the library are:

- Establish effective working relationships with superiors and associates

- Maintain effective working relationships with superiors and associates
- Establish effective working relationships with general public
- Maintain effective working relationships with general public
- Data entry (submitting grant reports)
- Carry out successful reference interview (assist patrons with)
- Conduct online research (assist patrons with)
- Conduct print research (assist patrons with)
- Find online reference materials (assist patrons with)
- Find print reference materials (assist patrons with)
- Select library materials (assist patrons with)
- Retrieve library materials (assist patrons with)
- Search online catalog (assist patrons with)
- Use of library's public access computers (assist patrons with)
- Develop programs to highlight the collection
- Develop programs to meet the needs of the public
- Develop themes for book displays
- Select materials for book display
- Market adult programs
- Room set up for events/programs
- Perform program logistics (handouts, notebooks, nametags)
- Coordinate with presenters
- Publicize results of program/event
- Perform program postmortem
- Shopping for materials/supplies for event/program
- Maintain supply inventory (for programs/events)
- Plan programs/events (event planning)
- Create schedule of events/programs
- Coordinate with departments
- Maintain library calendars (rooms, adult services)
- Identify community needs
- Identify how the library can fulfill community needs
- Make connections for those with a need and those who provide it
- Administer customer feedback surveys
- Assess marketing vehicles for effectiveness

- Perform monthly program assessment
- Recognize volunteers/presenters for their contribution
- Apply for grants
- Complete required post-mortem grant documentation
- Order coffee
- Pace yourself (effectively manage time)

We could have done a grouping at this time, but due to time constraints we went directly to the Four Attributes. This was and is acceptable since you don't have to do the grouping at any particular time much less at all. It can be useful to wait until after finding out which tasks are training requirements, simplifying the overall work.

Master Task Listing – Attribute Assessment (Business)

I've cut the list down to the first 25 for our purposes. And the results were:

Task	Frequency	Complexity of Task	Complexity to Learn	Criticality
Establish effective working relationships with superiors and associates	H	H	M	H
Maintain effective working relationships with superiors and associates	H	L	L	M
Establish effective working relationships with general public	H	M	M	H
Maintain effective working relationships with general public	H	L	L	H
Data entry (submitting grant reports)	M	L	L	L
Carry out successful reference interview	H	H	M	H
Conduct online research (assist patrons with)	H	M	M	M
Conduct print research (assist patrons with)	H	M	M	M

Task continued	Frequency	Complexity of Task	Complexity to Learn	Criticality
Find online reference materials for patrons	H	M	M	M
Find print reference materials for patrons	H	L	L	M
Select library materials (assist patrons with)	H	L	L	M
Retrieve library materials (assist patrons with)	H	L	L	M
Search online catalog (assist patrons with)	H	M	M	M
Assist patrons with library's public computers	H	L	L	M
Develop programs to highlight the collection	M	H	H	L
Develop programs to meet needs of the public	L	H	H	L
Develop themes for book displays	M	M	M	L
Select materials for book display	M	L	L	L
Market adult programs	L	M	H	M
Room set up for events/programs	L	L	L	L
Perform program logistics	L	L	L	L
Coordinate with presenters	L	L	L	H
Publicize results of program/event	M	L	L	L
Perform program postmortem	L	L	M	L
Shopping for materials/supplies for event/prgm	L	L	L	M

Figure 19, business task attributes

And the analysis recommends:

Task	Frequency	Compx of Task	Compx to Learn	Criticality	Tng Req't?	Knowledge Item?	Checklist?	Quality Check?	OJT?	Instructions	Formal Training?	JITT	Job Aids
Establish effective working relationships with superiors and associates	H	H	M	H	Y	Y	Y	Y	N	N	Y	N	N
Maintain effective working relationships with superiors and associates	H	L	L	M	N	N	Y	N	N	N	N	N	N
Establish effective working relationships with general public	H	M	M	H	Y	N	Y	Y	N	N	Y	N	N
Maintain effective working relationships with the public	H	L	L	H	N	N	Y	Y	N	N	N	N	N
Data entry (submitting grant reports)	M	L	L	L	N	N	N	N	N	N	N	N	N
Carry out successful reference interview	H	H	M	H	Y	Y	Y	Y	N	N	Y	N	N
Conduct online research (assist patrons with)	H	M	M	M	Y	N	Y	N	N	N	Y	N	N
Conduct print research (assist patrons with)	H	M	M	M	Y	N	Y	N	N	N	Y	N	N
Find online reference materials for patrons	H	M	M	M	Y	N	Y	N	N	N	Y	N	N
Find print reference materials for patrons	H	L	L	M	N	N	Y	N	N	N	N	N	N
Select library materials (assist patrons with)	H	L	L	M	N	N	Y	N	N	N	N	N	N
Retrieve library materials (assist patrons with)	H	L	L	M	N	N	Y	N	N	N	N	N	N
Search online catalog (assist patrons with)	H	M	M	M	Y	N	Y	N	N	N	Y	N	N
Use of library's public access computers (assist patrons with)	H	L	L	M	N	N	Y	N	N	N	N	N	N
Develop programs to highlight the collection	M	H	H	L	Y	Y	N	N	N	N	Y	N	N
Develop programs to meet the needs of the public	L	H	H	L	Y	Y	N	N	N	Y	Y	N	Y
Develop themes for book displays	M	M	M	L	Y	N	N	N	N	N	Y	N	N
Select materials for book display	M	L	L	L	N	N	N	N	N	N	N	N	N
Market adult programs	L	M	H	M	Y	Y	N	N	N	Y	Y	N	Y
Room set up for events/programs	L	L	L	L	N	N	N	N	N	N	N	N	Y
Perform program logistics (handouts, notebooks, nametags)	L	L	L	L	N	N	N	N	N	N	N	N	Y
Coordinate with presenters	L	L	L	H	N	N	Y	Y	N	N	N	Y	Y
Publicize results of program/event	M	L	L	L	N	N	N	N	N	N	N	N	N
Perform program postmortem	L	L	M	L	N	N	N	N	N	N	N	N	Y
Shopping for materials/supplies for event/program	L	L	L	M	N	N	Y	N	N	N	N	N	Y

Figure 20, business tasks analysis

Master Task Listing – Skill Assessment (Business)

Required level of ability to perform the tasks. Again, only showing the first twenty-five, but remember that we only need to assess the required skill for tasks which translated to be training requirements.

Task	Required Skill (supervisor)	Required Skill (Worker)	Final Score*
Establish effective working relationships with superiors and associates	4	3.5	4
Establish effective working relationships with general public	4	3	4
Carry out successful reference interview (assist patrons with)	4	4	4
Conduct online research (assist patrons with)	4	3	4
Conduct print research (assist patrons with)	4	3.5	4
Find online reference materials (assist patrons with)	4	4	4
Search online catalog (assist patrons with)	4	3	4
Develop programs to highlight the collection	3	3	3
Develop programs to meet the needs of the public	3	3	3
Develop themes for book displays	3	2.5	3
Market adult programs	3.5	2.75	3.5
Plan programs/events (event planning)	3	2.5	3
Create schedule of events/programs	2.5	3	3
Coordinate with departments	4	3	4
Maintain library calendars (rooms, adult services)	2.5	3	3
Identify community needs	4	4	4
Identify how the library can fulfill community needs	4	4	4
Make connections for those with a need and those who provide it	4	4	4
Pace yourself (effectively manage time)	4	3	4
Supervise Computer Lab staff	3.7	3.5	3.7
Supervise Information Desk staff	3.7	4	4
Supervise Adult Programming staff	3.7	4	4
Coach Computer Lab Staff	4	2.5	4
Coach Information Desk Staff	4	3.5	4
Coach Adult Programming Staff	4	4	4

Figure 21, business task requirement analysis

The next step is to analyze the current skill level of the person filling the position. But, in this case, as may be the case for you, there isn't a person currently filling the position. In which case, we stop here until we find a hire. You can use this tool for assessing your potential hires – even if you let those being looked at fill it in themselves. It can be a factor in your choice of hire – but remember, I don't recommend it be your top criteria.

Master Task Listing – Schedule (Business)

If you've read this book to this point (rather than having jumped to this chapter), you know that I don't the role causing a difference in how you would create a professional development plan. Exactly the same direction I provided for our Sport Example fits the business example. So if you've read the Sport example you can skip this section.

You can track the planned training any way you like – I tend to use spreadsheets because I'm familiar with them. The essential things to track are:

1. The task (easy one huh?)
2. The required skill level (so you can monitor improvement)
3. The skill level before training. This will hopefully change after each training session.
4. Priority. This is optional, but I find it helpful to clearly communicate with the trainee which tasks you feel are more important. This is especially useful with someone who is an alternate for a task (rather than the primary).
5. Training Start Date - planned and actual. This is important for showing your commitment as the supervisor and to make it clear that you expect the employee to work on these skills.
6. Training – what did you try? What training helped and which didn't work? You need to document these in the results.

7. Results – skill level after training. This helps for evaluating the effectiveness of the training provided. This provides insight into which types of training worked and which didn't. Granted each person is different; so what works for one may not work for another...but I'd prefer trying something that worked for one first, and avoid the training that didn't seem to help.

Plan Templates

A sample Microsoft Excel ® template for a development plan can be found on my website at mkknowledgebuilders.com under resources. It includes a visual mapping of the skill level of each trainee. It also includes a way to track skill and knowledge level evaluations and goals. One sheet is for training evaluation, the other is for scheduling and tracking training received. The use of the template is explained in the bonus material, "Checklist for creating a Personal Development Plan (from Position Planning to Personal Assessments)."

Chapter 3-10
Bonus Material

Checklist for creating a Personal Development Plan (from Position Planning to Personal Assessments)

You will have a positional development plan when you finish step 6. If you are developing a plan for a position with more than one worker, use the highest level identified. By completing the subsequent steps you will go from a positional plan to a personal (individual) development plan.

1. Identify roles for development plans
2. Identify the tasks which make up those roles
   a. Obtain and pull tasks from source documents
      i. Job descriptions
      ii. Job postings
      iii. Performance evaluations
      iv. Process definitions
   b. Elicit tasks from workers who currently fill the role
   c. Elicit tasks from supervisors of identified roles
3. Evaluate the four factors for each task, for each person filling the role
   a. Frequency the task is performed
   b. Criticality of the task (how important it is to get it right the first time)
   c. Complexity to perform the task
   d. Complexity to learn or teach the task
4. Review and adjust the evaluations with the supervisor
5. Determine results
   a. Which are training requirements
   b. Is supporting knowledge recommended?
   c. Is On-the-Job Training recommended?

        d. Is Just-in-Time Training recommended?
        e. Is a Training Aid recommended?
        f.   Is a Checklist recommended?
        g. Is a Quality Check recommended?
        h. Are Thorough Instructions recommended?
        i.   Is Formal Classroom Training recommended?

6. Review the Training Requirement Tasks for level of skill required to perform the job
   a. Have the supervisor assess the required skill levels
   b. Have the worker(s) assess the required skill levels
   c. Do a comparison.
      i. Spend no more than 3 minutes on tasks with conflicts
      ii. If no resolution is forth coming in 3 minutes take the higher of the two assessments

7. Review the Training Requirement Tasks for the current skill levels of each worker
   a. Have each worker assess his/her abilities to perform each task
   b. Have the supervisor assess each worker's ability to perform each task
   c. Do a comparison
      i. Spend no more than 3 minutes on tasks with conflicts
      ii. If no resolution is forth coming in 3 minutes take the lower of the two assessments

8. Identify deficiencies between the required level of skill and the current level
   a. Deficiencies exist where the required skill is higher than the current ability of the worker
   b. If the worker's skill is greater than the requirement, the deficiency is zero. If the worker's skill is equal to the requirement, the deficiency is also zero

9. Transfer all tasks with a deficiency to the personal development plan schedule of training
   a. Identify when the training is needed (when does the worker need to be able to perform the task at the required level of skill?)
   b. Identify sources for the training
10. Track training to task

Measures of Success

In my first book we introduced the concept of mature behaviors. Among them were Metrics, Professional Development Plans, and Strategic Planning. I covered metrics in my next book, because it was the most highly desired of the behaviors. I found (and continue to find) that most organizations want a viable metrics program above all other behaviors.

This is ironically in part because the organizations believe they already have a grasp of the other behaviors. With poor mission and vision statements they blithely go on with the thought that they have it all figured out. With poorly written goals they happily move forward with getting things done, rewarding themselves for being able to plan 12 months into the future. With a solid training budget in place they believe they fulfill the development needs of their staff because they spend the allotted amount for training each year.

But metrics, they don't fool themselves into believing they've conquered.

So, I started with metrics. An area with tons of opportunity and an audience ready to listen. The problem was (and is) that metrics are the most dangerous of the advanced behaviors. It *should* not be addressed early in an organization's maturation. Strategic Planning and Professional Development are both better behaviors to start with. As in Metrics: How to Improve Business Results, these two mature behaviors belong to the lower two quadrants – Leader's and Worker's Viewpoints, respectively.

Metrics creates Fear, Uncertainty, and Doubt (FUD) because no matter your intentions, the workforce will only hear that you seek to measure them. Regardless of the truth, the FUD will make it impossible for them to hear it.

In contrast, when you work on a real mission, vision and goals the workforce hears the direction you want the organization to move in. And when the workforce hears that you want to help them develop professionally, they will hear that you care.

There may be no better goal for a leader to achieve than to help another succeed. There may be no clearer way to achieve this goal than to help create a realistic, useful, and usable professional development plan.

One last thought

While I started with metrics, you shouldn't. You should start with your mission, vision, and a strategic plan. Along with these, feel free to jump into professional development planning. The next mature behavior I cover will be Vision Setting. It's an equally safe opportunity for improvement, and it's the one I enjoy the most.

Other Books by Martin Klubeck

Metrics: How to Improve Key Business Results

A short course on using metrics to improve your organization quickly.

Paperback: 370 pages
Publisher: Apress; 1 edition (Dec 6, 2011)
ISBN-13: 978-1430237266

Executive leadership, boards of directors, management, and customers are all asking for data-based decisions. As a result, many managers, professionals, and change agents are asked to develop metrics, but have no clear idea of how to produce meaningful ones. Wouldn't it be great to have a simple explanation of how to collect, analyze, report, and use measurements to improve your organization?

Metrics: How to Improve Key Business Results provides that explanation and the tools you'll need to make your organization more effective. Not only does the book explain the "why" of metrics, but it walks you through a step-by-step process for creating a report card that provides a clear picture of organizational health and how well you satisfy customer needs.

Metrics will help you to measure the right things, the right way—the first time. No wasted effort, no chasing data.

Find it at Amazon, Barnes&Noble, and quality bookstores everywhere.